A SHORT
HISTORY
OF BRITAIN
IN INFOGRAPHICS

RAY HAMILTON

A SHORT HISTORY OF BRITAIN IN INFOGRAPHICS

An Hachette UK Company
www.hachette.co.uk

Summersdale Publishers Ltd
Part of Octopus Publishing Group Limited
Carmelite House
50 Victoria Embankment
LONDON
EC4Y 0DZ

www.summersdale.com

Printed and bound in the Czech Republic

ISBN: 978-1-78685-029-4

Substantial discounts on bulk quantities of Summersdale books are available to corporations, professional associations and other organisations. For details contact general enquiries: telephone: +44 (0) 1243 771107 or email: enquiries@summersdale.com.

A SHORT
HISTORY
OF BRITAIN
IN INFOGRAPHICS

RAY HAMILTON

Other books by Ray Hamilton (all published by Summersdale)

Knowledge: Stuff You Ought to Know (2016)

M25: A Circular Tour of the London Orbital (2015)

Trains: A Miscellany (2015)

The Joy of Golf (2014)

The Joy of Cycling (2013)

Le Tour de France: The Greatest Race in Cycling History (2013)

Military Quotations: Stirring Words of War and Peace (2012)

Contents

Acknowledgements

My thanks to Summersdale Publishers for the opportunity to write this book and to Chris Turton in particular for his very helpful input and for being such a pleasure to work with again. Thanks also to Emily Kearns for her sharp-eyed copy-editing and to my wife Karen for first-reading everything I write.

Note on dates used in this book

Just in case you haven't come across the BCE and CE dating convention before, let me explain. We used always to say BC (before Christ) and AD (Anno Domini), but the world's historians decided to standardise their dating conventions a bit, which has the added benefit of being a bit more inclusive from a faith point of view. So now we can use Before Common Era (BCE) and Common Era (CE) instead, which is what I have done in this book, because I'm a modern kind of a guy. No conversions will be necessary, because BCE equates exactly with BC and CE equates exactly with AD.

Note on the order of the home nations

For fear of displaying a preference for one home nation over another, I have referred throughout this book to England, Northern Ireland, Scotland and Wales in alphabetical order.

Introduction

Only by understanding our history can we fully grasp what it means to be British today, what it means to be English, Northern Irish, Scottish or Welsh within the United Kingdom of Great Britain and Northern Ireland, whether we think our personal ancestors have always lived here or not (they haven't). Only by understanding how we gathered our language, habits and cuisine from the far corners of the earth can we begin to understand the marvellous melting pot we live in today.

We can be proud of the astonishing array of inventions and products we have given to the world over the centuries, and it is fair to say that we have always punched above our weight on the world stage for such a small nation (think British Empire, Industrial Revolution, Olympic Games). We even invented the weather, which is why ours has always been more interesting than anyone else's. Why else would we talk about it so much?

This book will look at all those things and more, at what has brought us to where we are today, starting with our ancient history and working our way through centuries of achievement, glory and, let's not forget, a fair amount of war and infamy.

CHAPTER 1

WHAT'S IN A NAME?

Before we start, let's consider who we are. Much confusion surrounds the terminology of the country we call home and you may quite correctly consider yourself to live in the United Kingdom, the UK, Great Britain or Britain, all of which are widely used shorthand for the United Kingdom of Great Britain and Northern Ireland, which is our formal and internationally recognised title. We then further complicate matters by living more specifically in England, Northern Ireland, Scotland or Wales. But how did we end up with so many names?

United Kingdom

9

Britain

Great Britain

The word Britain derives from *Britannia*, the Latin word applied by the Romans to describe the territory of the Britons, the Iron Age tribes who inhabited what is now England and southern Scotland at the time of the Roman invasion in 43 CE.

In 1707 the Acts of Union brought England (which included Wales at the time) and Scotland together as the Kingdom of Great Britain, the first time that name had formally existed. The 'Great' referred to the larger geographical size of the new country, and was never intended to serve as a pompous declaration of our greatness.

United Kingdom of Great Britain and Ireland

The 1800 Acts of Union brought the Kingdom of Great Britain and the Kingdom of Ireland together as the United Kingdom of Great Britain and Ireland, which was the first formal and lasting reference to a United Kingdom.

IRELAND

United Kingdom of Great Britain and Northern Ireland

The United Kingdom of Great Britain and Northern Ireland has only existed since 1922, when it succeeded the United Kingdom of Great Britain and Ireland following the partition of Ireland.

Northern Ireland

The name of (Northern) Ireland derives from a Gaelic goddess called Ériu, which later became the modern Irish word Éire.

Scotland

Scotia was originally a Roman name for Ireland, but the use of the name changed in the Middle Ages to refer to the territory north of the Firth of Forth (which the Romans had in fact referred to as Caledonia).

England

The name of England derives from the Angles, the Germanic tribe who invaded Britain in the fifth century.

Wales

The name Wales derives from the Germanic word *Wealas*, meaning 'foreigners', which was how the Anglo-Saxons used to refer to the inhabitants of the lands of the Celtic Britons.

British Isles

The British Isles is a geographical term that includes each and every island of the United Kingdom and of Ireland, including, therefore, the whole of the mainland of Great Britain and the whole of the island of Ireland. There are over 6,000 smaller islands, the vast majority being uninhabited, the most populated being Portsea Island, Isle of Wight, Jersey, Isle of Man, Anglesey and Guernsey.

The islands were established in their current form about 12,000 years ago, primarily as a result of the deglaciation that occurred at the end of the Ice Age.

SCOTLAND

IRELAND

ENGLAND

WALES

Union Jack

Also referred to as the Union Flag, the Union Jack was designed to reflect the union of Great Britain and Ireland that had been brought about by the 1800 Acts of Union. It is an amalgamation of the red cross of St George (representing England), the white saltire of St Andrew (representing Scotland) and the red saltire of St Patrick (representing Ireland). As Wales was a part of England at the time, poor St David was left out in the cold.

CHAPTER 2

BRITAIN THROUGH THE AGES

It is close to a thousand years since our island nation was last invaded, by the Normans on that occasion and by the Vikings and Romans before them. After living under French influence for a while, Britain then suffered centuries-long strife as warring factions fought for the throne or for religious dominance. Eventually united as a kingdom, the country went on to build an empire that spanned the globe and subsequently brought many of those it had colonised home. Britons even became Europeans for a while, before deciding on 23 June 2016, for better or worse, that they would rather be an island nation again. Let's start at the beginning, though, with our less-than-civilised ancestors.

Coin from the reign of Richard III

BEING INVADED

All the tribes of Britain ever wanted to do was fight amongst themselves, but one invader after another had bigger ideas for them. One by one, the Romans, Angles, Jutes, Saxons, Franks, Frisians, Vikings and Normans turned up and took advantage of a vulnerability brought on by the inherent inability of the British tribes to join together for the common good.

Ancient Britons
(600 BCE–84 CE)

Our early ancestors were mostly Celtic tribes who lived and fought each other in Britain throughout the Iron Age, until the Romans arrived and at least gave them a common enemy for a while.

CELTIC HIGHLIGHTS

The Celts dominated Britain from the well-defended hill forts they built everywhere they went.

As fierce warriors who often preferred to go into battle naked as a sign of personal bravery, they were surely the cause of many a nightmare within the ranks of the Roman centurions.

Queen Boudicca (or Boadicea) was the most famous Celtic warrior of all, rebelling against the Roman invasion where many male warriors had failed, and destroying several important Roman towns.

The Celts were also skilled metalworkers, their art still recognisable today by their trademark patterns.

Led by Druid priests, they shared common pagan beliefs, considering the oak tree to be sacred and building the mysterious stone circles like the one at Stonehenge.

The many different tribes spoke similar languages, including Scottish Gaelic, Welsh and Irish Gaelic.

Under Roman rule (43–410 CE)

The Roman empire was built on the premise that it was time to civilise barbarians everywhere and, in the case of Britain they certainly had their work cut out. After a couple of failed invasion attempts by Julius Caesar, the Emperor Claudius finally succeeded in 43 CE, heralding the start of almost 400 years of Roman rule.

ROMAN HIGHLIGHTS

It took the Romans about 40 years to finally conquer present-day England and Wales. They finally gave up trying to conquer what is now Scotland, so they built Hadrian's Wall to keep the Caledonians out instead.

They built magnificent towns, notably at Camulodunum (Colchester), Londinium (London), Verulamium (St Albans) and Aquae Sulis (Bath), and built perfectly straight roads between them.

They introduced shops and offices, marketplaces, running water and public baths, i.e. civilisation as we know it today.

After the Roman garrison on Hadrian's Wall rebelled in 367 CE, the tribes of Britain took advantage and overwhelmed the Romans on many fronts. It proved to be the beginning of the end for Roman Britain.

The Anglo-Saxons (410–1066)

In the fifth century, with the Romans out of the way, a number of northern European peoples saw a gap in the invasion market and arrived in Britain in their droves. Angles, Saxons, Jutes, Franks and Frisians all sailed across to push the indigenous Celtic tribes north and west into Wales, Ireland and Scotland. Those left behind in England became Anglo-Saxons under Germanic or Danish rule.

ANGLO-SAXON HIGHLIGHTS

The Anglo-Saxons were initially adept farmers who lived in rural villages in northern Europe.

After they got good at building ships, they sailed them to distant lands in search of ever greener pastures.

They ruled Britain for over 600 years, although hardly by Roman standards, because culture and commerce were slowly replaced with disease and violence.

They brought with them Bible translations and a passion for epic poetry, which resulted in the writing of *Beowulf*.

Benedictine monk the Venerable Bede provided an invaluable account of life under the Anglo-Saxons in his work *The Ecclesiastical History of the English People*, completed in 731.

In 757 a civil war resulted in Offa of Mercia declaring himself ruler of all England and constructing a long-distance earthwork (Offa's Dyke) to protect against Welsh raids.

At the mercy of the Vikings (793–1066)

The Vikings wreaked havoc around Britain since the time of their first raid on Lindisfarne in 793 all the way through to 1066. No town or village in England, Ireland, Scotland, Wales or even the Isle of Man was safe from their murderous intent in all that time.

VIKING HIGHLIGHTS

866 – The Vikings took control of Jorvik (York) and turned it into the second biggest city in England after London.

878 – King Alfred, the Saxon King of Wessex, defeated the Vikings at the Battle of Edington.

886 – Alfred retook London but conceded the area of the Danelaw (all of England above Watling Street, the Roman road from Chester to London) to Guthrum, the Viking ruler of East Anglia.

10th century – Once the Vikings had what they wanted, i.e. most of Britain, they settled down for a while, allowing the Anglo-Saxons to learn much about farming, trading and shipbuilding from them.

927 – The Anglo-Saxons finally succeeded in converging England's diverse kingdoms into a single country under King Æthelstan.

1012 – King Æthelred the Unready tried to buy off the Vikings ahead of a further invasion with what became known as Danegeld, but Sweyn Forkbeard attacked anyway and for a while the Vikings had control of the whole of England.

Being French for a while (1066–1154)

Many of the Normans who conquered Britain in 1066 had originally arrived in Normandy from Scandinavia, i.e. as Vikings, but their language and culture by then were much closer to what we know today as French. In no time at all, that language and that culture were the main ones to be found across England, including present-day Wales.

NORMAN HIGHLIGHTS

1028 – Birth of William the Conqueror (or William I), a direct descendant of Rollo, the first Viking to turn native and help the French defend themselves against the raids of his own brother Ragnar Lodbrok.

1066 – After victory at the Battle of Hastings, William was crowned at Westminster Abbey on Christmas Day 1066, the ceremony being conducted entirely in Norman French, the language of England for the next 300 years.

1070 – Construction of Windsor Castle started.

1078 – The original Tower of London (the White Tower) was erected.

1080 – The Normans built a fortification they named 'New Castle upon the Tyne' to stop King Malcolm III of Scotland constantly invading England, constantly being driven back and constantly promising not to do it again.

1086 – The Domesday Book was introduced to determine who owned which land and to impose harsh taxes accordingly, leading landowners to compare it to the Last Judgement, or Doomsday.

1100 – William II, son of William I and crowned following his father's death in 1087, was suspiciously killed by an arrow while out hunting.

1100–54 – The reigns of the third and fourth Norman kings, Henry I (1100–35) and Stephen (1135–54), were plagued by civil war as neither had a strong claim to the throne.

PLANTAGENETS AND TUDORS

The next 500 years under the Plantagenets and Tudors were beset with religious fervour, war, civil strife, rebellion and plague, and provided our history with some of its most colourful characters.

The Plantagenets (1154–1485)

The Plantagenets carried on where the Normans left off, ruling England in French until the Hundred Years' War with France (1337–1453) made that a bit awkward and the English language started to make a bit of a comeback. The Wars of the Roses (1455–1485) later pitched the rival Plantagenet Houses of York and Lancaster against one other for the post-French control of England.

PLANTAGENET HIGHLIGHTS

1170 – Henry II had Thomas Becket, the Archbishop of Canterbury, murdered for banging on about the Church being more powerful than the State.

1189–92 – Richard I (the Lionheart) played a prominent role in the Third Crusade to the Holy Land, but that may have been mostly an excuse to get away from England. In the ten years he reigned (1189–99), he spent less than six months in the country, spoke not a word of English and left instructions for his heart to be buried in France when he died.

1215 – The Magna Carta was signed by King John, finally limiting the powers of the crown and establishing the foundation of British law.

1294–95 – Edward I, known as Longshanks on account of his height, ruthlessly quashed a Welsh rebellion led by Madog ap Llywelyn.

1305 – The Scottish knight William Wallace was hanged, drawn and quartered by Edward I as punishment for inflicting a notable victory against the English at the Battle of Stirling Bridge in 1297.

1314 – Robert the Bruce, King of Scots, exacted some revenge by defeating Edward II at the Battle of Bannockburn.

1346–53 – The Black Death, a bubonic plague that turned the skin of its victims black, reduced the population of England by a third.

1483 – The 12-year-old Edward V and his younger brother Prince Richard, aka the Princes in the Tower, were allegedly disposed of in the Tower of London so that their bad uncle Richard III could be king instead.

The Hundred Years' War (1337–1453)

The Hundred Years' War between France and England raged for 116 years, the overtime being needed primarily because the Black Death almost wiped out both armies early on, which meant that both sides had to grow some new soldiers until they were old enough to be killed. The most significant events of the Hundred Years' War were as follows:

1346 After introducing the longbow and enlisting the help of his son the Black Prince, Edward III beat a much larger French army at Crécy.

1415 Henry V of England attacked once more unto the breach and secured a famous victory at Agincourt, despite the English forces again being outnumbered by the opposition.

1431 The teenage peasant girl Joan of Arc surprised everyone by helping French forces to break the English siege of Orléans. She was burned at the stake two years later by the English, but the victory she inspired was the turning point of the war in France's favour.

1453 The French finally emerged victorious and England was left with only Calais and the Channel Islands to show for over a hundred years of warfare.

The Wars of the Roses (1455–85)

The Wars of the Roses saw the rival Plantagenet Houses of York and Lancaster fight it out for the English crown, and were so named on account of the heraldic badges of the two houses, that of the House of Lancaster being a red rose and that of the House of York being a white rose.

1455 – The wars started with a revolt led by Richard, Duke of York against the Lancastrian rule of Henry VI.

1486 – Henry Tudor (now Henry VII) united the two houses by marrying Elizabeth of York and starting the Tudor dynasty to avoid the contentious nomenclature of Lancaster or York.

1461 – The House of York finally gained power after winning the Battle of Towton under Edward IV.

1485 – The wars ended when the Lancastrian Henry Tudor defeated the Yorkist Richard III at the Battle of Bosworth Field.

1483 – Edward IV died and was succeeded by Richard III.

The Tudors (1485–1603)

Henry VII returned England to prosperity and stability following the unsettling period of the Wars of the Roses, leaving a fortune and a relatively sound system of government to his son, Henry VIII, in 1509. Things started to get a bit messy again after that.

TUDOR HIGHLIGHTS

For the whole of the sixteenth century you could be tortured on the rack, burned at the stake, decapitated, disembowelled or hanged, drawn and quartered for any of the following offences:

- Being too Catholic
- Being too Protestant
- Being too French
- Being too Scottish
- Looking a bit too longingly at the wrong person in the royal court
- Failing to produce a son and heir in timely fashion

1509–47 – Reign of Henry VIII, who worked his way through six wives and churlishly dissolved the monasteries after the Pope refused to recognise the annulment of his marriage to Catherine of Aragon.

1547–53 – The sickly Edward VI became king at the age of nine and died six years later at the ripe old age of 15. His advisors had tried to get him married to the teenage Mary, Queen of Scots, but her advisors had preferred to align with France.

1553–58 – Mary I (Bloody Mary) executed a teenage rival for the throne (Lady Jane Grey, who had been de facto queen for nine days), burned Protestants on a fearsome scale, and just stopped short of having her half-sister (the future Elizabeth I) executed. She did make a nice cocktail, though.

1558–1603 – Elizabeth I reinstated Protestantism, encouraged exploration of the New World by the likes of Francis Drake and Walter Raleigh, allowed the arts to flourish (Shakespeare was a particular favourite) and drank two pints of beer for breakfast.

1587 – Mary, Queen of Scots, got her head chopped off for being too Catholic, too French (she had in fact been Queen of France for a while and French was her first language) and too conspiratorial.

1588 – The Spanish Armada was defeated by a combination of English ships and English weather.

The six wives of Henry VIII

Here are the results of Henry VIII's six marriages (with dates of marriage in parentheses):

 Catherine of Aragon (1509–33) Produced the future Mary I, but had to go after failing to produce a son and heir.

 Anne Boleyn (1533–36) Produced the future Elizabeth I, but also failed to bear a son and was allegedly a bit too popular with the boys around court in any event.

 Jane Seymour (1536–37) Lost her life giving birth to the future Edward VI, and would otherwise probably have lived happily ever after with Henry after giving him the male heir he always wanted.

 Anne of Cleves (1540) Described by Henry as the 'mare of Flanders', she was removed for being insufficiently pleasing to the eye.

 Catherine Howard (1540–42) Another one who allegedly put it about too much at court, which was so embarrassing it earned her a beheading.

 Catherine Parr (1543–47) After three other marriages of her own, she managed Henry so well that she survived long enough to outlive him.

 beheaded died divorced (annulled)  survived

UNITING THE KINGDOM UNDER THE STUARTS AND GEORGIANS

The next couple of hundred years saw Britain start to come together as a united kingdom, albeit against an ongoing backdrop of war and rebellion at home and abroad. French influence would become a thing of the past, only to be replaced by an equally strong German hold on the country.

The Stuarts and the English Civil War (1603–1714)

The Stuart dynasty kicked off when James VI of Scotland (the son of Mary, Queen of Scots) also became James I of England. Over the next hundred years the people suffered ongoing religious strife, civil war, plague, fire and general misery, but things improved for a while after Charles II returned from exile in France to reintroduce some much-needed debauchery.

STUART HIGHLIGHTS

1605   On 5 November, Catholic dissidents, including Guy Fawkes, tried to blow up the House of Lords.

1620   The puritanically Protestant Pilgrim Fathers set off from Plymouth, beginning a long period of migration to the New World.

1642–51 The English Civil War resulted from rebellion against the tyrannical rule of King Charles I and pitched the Parliamentary Roundheads of Oliver Cromwell against the Royalist Cavaliers of the king.

1645	Following the indecisive Battle of Edgehill in 1642, the Parliamentarians had by now secured the upper hand with decisive victories at Marston Moor (1644) and Naseby (1645).
1649	Charles I had his head removed.
1651	The Parliamentarians won overall victory following the Battle of Worcester.
1651–60	Charles II was forced to live in exile in France.
1651–58	After also subjugating Ireland and Scotland with his New Model Army, Oliver Cromwell ruled as Lord Protector of the Commonwealth of England, Scotland and Ireland until his death. Even Christmas was banned under his fun-hating regime.
1660	The monarchy was restored when Charles II returned from exile in France. Christmas was immediately reinstated, along with general merriment and debauchery at court.
1665–66	The Great Plague of London spoiled the ongoing party a bit. It killed about 100,000 people, a quarter of the London population, being transmitted through a bite from an infected rat flea. Charles II and his family ran off to Salisbury in order to avoid London like the plague.
1689	William III of Orange and his wife Queen Mary II restored some sobriety to court, agreeing to the Bill of Rights to limit the powers of the crown, allow Parliament to hold regular elections and prevent Catholics from acceding to the throne.
1707	The Acts of Union brought Scotland and England together to form the Kingdom of Great Britain.

Great Fire of London in numbers

In 1666, the Great Fire of London wreaked havoc and destroyed St Paul's Cathedral but, on the plus side, it put paid to any chance of the Great Plague flaring up again.

2
cost in shillings of hiring a cart before the fire started

4
number of days it took to sweep through the city from the bakery in Pudding Lane where it started

6 verified number of deaths

87
number of parish churches destroyed

40
cost in pounds of hiring a cart at the height of the fire (everybody wanted to get their goods out of the city)

1,250°C
temperature of the fire

17,000
number of inhabitants left homeless (out of a total of 80,000 Londoners)

13,000
number of houses burned down

The Georgians (1714–1837)

The royal House of Hanover began when George I turned up to rule Britain in 1714 speaking only German. The so-called Georgian period of the four Georges plus William IV (who was George IV's younger brother) saw many wars and much empire building.

GEORGIAN HIGHLIGHTS

When Queen Anne died in 1714 without any surviving children, George I got the job as her nearest Protestant relative, jumping over more than 50 closer blood relatives who were Catholic and therefore prohibited from inheriting the throne.

1721–42: Robert Walpole served as Britain's first prime minister for more than 20 years, a remarkable achievement made possible by his adroit handling of the House of Commons on the one hand and two kings on the other (George I and II).

1745: Charles Edward Stuart, aka Bonnie Prince Charlie, aka the Young Pretender, had one last go at restoring the Catholic Stuarts to the throne, but he lost at Culloden Moor to the Duke of Cumberland and escaped over the sea to Skye disguised as a maid. His followers were systematically butchered by Cumberland.

1756–63: The Seven Years' War was the conflict that resulted in Britain taking control of Spanish Florida, French Canada (after General James Wolfe took Quebec) and Bengal in East India (mainly thanks to the efforts of the British commander Robert Clive).

1775–83: The American Revolutionary War (aka the American War of Independence) started as a rebellion against unjust British taxes and escalated into a drive for independence, an objective that was ultimately successful thanks to the French pitching in with the newly declared United States of America.

1812: Spencer Perceval became the only British prime minister to be assassinated, shot inside the House of Commons by disgruntled commoner John Bellingham.

1792–1815: The French Revolutionary Wars (1792–1802) and subsequent Napoleonic Wars (1803–15) saw Britain and its allies trying to teach Republican France a lesson by restoring the French monarchy, whereupon Napoleon Bonaparte set about conquering the whole of Europe to teach it to mind its own business.

Why Napoleon didn't like the British:

- He suffered two heavy naval defeats at the hands of Horatio Nelson, namely the Battle of the Nile in 1798 and the Battle of Trafalgar in 1805.

- He invaded Russia in 1812 because they had failed to support a trade embargo against Britain, but forgot just how cold the winter in Russia can get (of the 500,000 soldiers he took with him, only about 27,000 returned).

- During his exile on the Italian island of Elba (1814–15), the British let him have a small navy and hold lavish parties, but he still got depressed and tried to commit suicide.

- He finally met his Waterloo at the Battle of Waterloo in 1815, at the hands of the Duke of Wellington and the Prussian Field Marshal Gebhard Leberecht von Blücher.

- When he knew he was dying on the South Atlantic island of St Helena in 1821, he accused his British captors of having poisoned him.

THE POWERFUL VICTORIANS AND SHORT-LIVED EDWARDIANS

The Industrial Revolution in Britain had a ready overseas market in the burgeoning British Empire. It was also a time of exploration and invention, but it wasn't without its conflicts at home and abroad and the common people remained more concerned about the appalling quality of their lives than the size of the empire.

The Victorian age (1837–1901)

Although America had been lost, Victorian Britain still had Canada, Australia, New Zealand, India and many parts of Africa and the Caribbean. Victoria was said to reign over an empire on which the sun never set, ruling over a quarter of the world's population and landmass.

VICTORIAN HIGHLIGHTS

Victorian firsts included the postage stamp (1840), free schooling (1870), trade unions (1871), the telephone (1876) and Greenwich Mean Time (1884), which unified time across the whole country for the first time.

The monarchy's influence waned during the Victorian era and there was a shift in power from the House of Lords to the House of Commons.

During the Victorian age Britain became the industrial powerhouse of the world, producing vast quantities of steel, coal, iron and textiles, and huge numbers of steamships and steam locomotives.

The Crimean War (1853–56) started as an argument between Russian Orthodox monks and French Catholics over the Holy Land, but that didn't stop Britain getting involved. It was notable for military incompetence, including the infamous Charge of the Light Brigade at Balaclava.

Queen Victoria never recovered from the early loss of her German husband (and cousin) Prince Albert, spending the final 40 years of her life in mourning. Prime Minister Benjamin Disraeli did coax her back into public life to a certain extent by reminding her that she had a worldwide empire to preside over when she got a minute.

The so-called Colonial Wars that coincided with Victoria's reign generally involved putting down resistance by Britain's seemingly ungrateful colonies:

1837: Upper and Lower
    Canada Rebellions
1839–42: First Anglo–Afghan War
1839–42: First Opium War
1856–60: Second Opium War
1878–71: Second Anglo–Afghan War
1845–46: First Anglo–Sikh War
1845–72: New Zealand Wars
1846–79: Xhosa Wars
1848–49: Second Anglo–Sikh War

1852–53: Second Anglo–Burmese War
1856–57: Anglo–Persian War
1868: Abyssinian Expedition
1879: Anglo–Zulu War
1880–81: Basuto War
1880–81: First Boer War
1884–85: Nile Expedition
1899–1902: Second Boer War
1900: Ashanti Uprising, aka the
    War of the Golden Stool

Victorian industry in numbers

10
minimum age for a child to get a job in a coal mine

2,000
approximate number of steam locomotives produced each year

30
percentage of British exports that went to the countries of the British Empire

26,000
number of telephones in use within a year of Alexander Graham Bell filing the patent

8
minimum age for a child to get a job in a factory

18,600
miles of railway track built in Britain by 1900

5 million
tons of steel produced annually by 1900

50
percentage of the rural population that moved to towns and cities to find work in the factories

33
percentage of the world's total manufactured exports produced in Britain

100,000
number of industrial steam engines at work throughout Britain

9 million
tons of iron produced annually by 1900

Served them right for being naughty

Between 1788 and 1868 Britain dumped about 160,000 unwanted convicts in the penal colony it had set up at Botany Bay in New South Wales, Australia. Some of the crimes that were actually punished by transportation included:

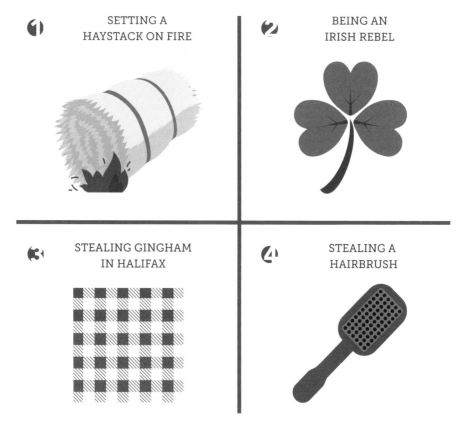

1. SETTING A HAYSTACK ON FIRE

2. BEING AN IRISH REBEL

3. STEALING GINGHAM IN HALIFAX

4. STEALING A HAIRBRUSH

Crimes punishable by death in Britain over that same period included:

 impersonating a Chelsea pensioner

 living with gypsies for a month

 strong evidence of malice in children aged 7–14

The Edwardians (1901–10)

The Edwardian era was a short-lived one, primarily because the Prince of Wales had had to wait such a long time for his mother to shuffle off her mortal coil.

EDWARDIAN HIGHLIGHTS

As the future King Edward VII, the Prince of Wales enjoyed a playboy lifestyle while waiting for his mother's reign to finally end. He particularly enjoyed horse racing, shooting, fine wines, actresses (especially Lillie Langtry) and other men's wives.

The House of Hanover ended when Edward acceded to the throne, because he favoured the House of Saxe-Coburg and Gotha after the duchy of his late father Prince Albert.

As monarch, Edward modernised the armed forces and personally promoted the Entente Cordiale signed with France in 1904 to rule out future wars between England and France.

THE WORLD WARS

World War One (1914–18)

World War One brought the horrors of trench warfare to northern Europe, including poison gas, shell shock, mutilation and widespread disease, but it also spread death and destruction as far away as Africa, China, the Middle East and the Pacific Ocean. Britain would play a huge part across the globe because it was able to summon troops throughout its vast empire, and in 1917 George V wisely changed the name of the British royal family from Saxe-Coburg and Gotha to Windsor.

WORLD WAR ONE IN APPROXIMATE NUMBERS

16 million

total deaths by the time the Allies (the British Empire, the Russian Empire, France, Italy, Japan, USA) defeated the Central Powers (Germany, Austria-Hungary, Bulgaria, Ottoman Empire) in 1918

1 million

total British deaths (including civilians) throughout the conflict

93

as war was fought by air for the first time, this was the average life expectancy (in hours) of a British pilot

2.77 million

number of conscripts to British armed forces after Prime Minister David Lloyd George introduced conscription in 1916

3 million

Commonwealth troops who rallied to support Britain, half of whom were Indian

420,000

British casualties at the Battle of the Somme, over the five months that it took the Allies to advance just 5 miles. It was the bloodiest conflict in British history

4 million

number of fresh troops supplied when the USA entered the war in 1917 after German U-boats had attacked its ships

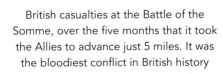

890,000

number of women who helped the war effort by working in munitions factories

5,000

number of merchant ships sunk by German U-boats. They were so successful at cutting off supply lines that Britain considered surrendering in 1916

2 million

men who responded to Lord Kitchener's call for volunteers in the first two years of the war

The inter-war years (1918–39)

It never takes long for the euphoria of victory to fade and for the harsh realities of a post-conflict world to hit home. Life in Britain after World War One was no exception, although some progress was finally made on women's rights.

1918: British women over the age of 30 who owned property were given the right to vote. The following year Lady Astor became the first female MP in Britain, and by 1928 all women over 21 were eligible to vote.

1918–20: The Spanish Flu pandemic killed over a quarter of a million British people and over 50 million people worldwide, over three times the number killed in World War One.

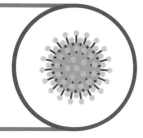

1919: The massacre that took place at the holy shrine of Amritsar in India at the hands of the British added fuel to the separatist movement that would ultimately lead to independence.

1922: The formation of the Irish Free State, which comprised 26 of the 32 counties of Ireland, resulted from the Irish War of Independence (1919–21). The remaining six counties exercised their right to opt out and formed the country of Northern Ireland.

1931: The British Commonwealth was established as the British Empire began to be dismantled. Australia, New Zealand, South Africa, Canada, Newfoundland and the Irish Free State were founder members.

1933: Adolf Hitler came to power in Germany, still smarting from the humiliation of the peace terms imposed at the end of World War One and hell-bent on revenge. Britain pursued diplomacy as he pursued rearmament on an unprecedented scale. World War Two was fast becoming inevitable.

1936: George VI came to the throne after his brother Edward VIII abdicated in favour of marrying the twice-divorced American socialite Wallis Simpson.

World War Two (1939–45)

The world was barely getting over World War One by the time the death and destruction of World War Two once more reduced it to its knees. Man's inhumanity to man would find new levels and Britain would once more punch way above its weight.

SIGNIFICANT FACTS ABOUT WORLD WAR TWO

1939	1940	1940
Prime Minister Neville Chamberlain declared war on Germany on 3 September following Germany's invasion of Poland.	Winston Churchill took over when it became clear that Neville Chamberlain was out of his depth as a wartime prime minister. Within weeks Churchill had raised morale with the successful evacuation of British troops from Dunkirk.	Despite being heavily outnumbered, the RAF defeated the Luftwaffe to win the Battle of Britain, ultimately resulting in Hitler calling off Operation Sea Lion, the code name for his planned invasion of Britain.

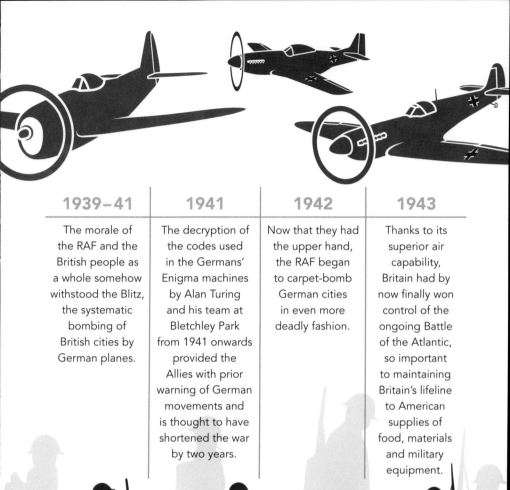

1939–41	1941	1942	1943
The morale of the RAF and the British people as a whole somehow withstood the Blitz, the systematic bombing of British cities by German planes.	The decryption of the codes used in the Germans' Enigma machines by Alan Turing and his team at Bletchley Park from 1941 onwards provided the Allies with prior warning of German movements and is thought to have shortened the war by two years.	Now that they had the upper hand, the RAF began to carpet-bomb German cities in even more deadly fashion.	Thanks to its superior air capability, Britain had by now finally won control of the ongoing Battle of the Atlantic, so important to maintaining Britain's lifeline to American supplies of food, materials and military equipment.

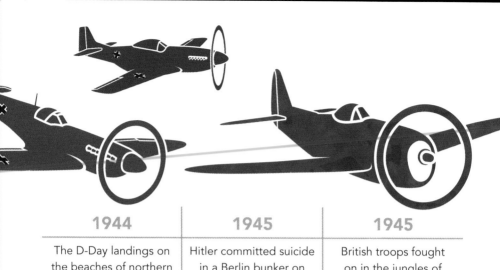

1944

The D-Day landings on the beaches of northern France on 6 June 1944 proved decisive as they allowed the Allies, now supported by the Americans, to move towards Germany from the west while the Russians did likewise from the east.

1945

Hitler committed suicide in a Berlin bunker on 30 April and the war in Europe ended on 8 May.

1945

British troops fought on in the jungles of South East Asia for another three months, until Japan finally rued the day it had attacked Pearl Harbor in 1941. Japan's unconditional surrender on 15 August came only after the USA had dropped atomic bombs on Hiroshima and Nagasaki and World War Two was finally over.

WORLD WAR TWO IN NUMBERS

20,000
number of privately owned guns donated by the public to the Home Guard

1,470,000
number of British people (mostly women and children) evacuated from vulnerable cities

746
U-boats destroyed

2,640
ships sunk in the Atlantic by 800 U-boats

2,870,000
Allied military and support forces deployed on D-Day

132,500
number of aircraft produced in Britain during the war

45,000,000
worldwide civilian casualties

15,000,000
worldwide military casualties

1mil.
number of volunteers who served in the Home Guard

383,600
British military casualties

67,100
British civilian casualties

34
number of enemy aircraft destroyed by British RAF pilot James 'Johnnie' Johnson, the most scored by any Allied flyer

MODERN BRITAIN

Britain emerged from World War Two victorious, but bankrupt and in huge debt to the USA. Reforms were nonetheless pushed through in the hope of providing the post-war population with appropriate education, employment, pensions and cradle-to-grave healthcare.

Britain has since navigated its way through widespread social change, population growth, obsessive consumerism, a huge multicultural influx, troubles at home and abroad, a tricky relationship with the European Union, growing nationalism and a sea change in technology.

Welcoming the world

The British Commonwealth morphed into the Commonwealth of Nations after the war, and the British government advertised for immigrants to come and bolster the workforce that had been depleted by war. The citizens of Ireland, the West Indies and the Indian subcontinent responded in great numbers, but they were by no means alone.

- In 1948 the first immigrants arrived from the West Indies, adding spice to British cuisine and reggae, ska and calypso beats to British music. Their cultural impact is still celebrated today at the annual Notting Hill Carnival in London.

- The Irishmen who helped rebuild Britain in the aftermath of the war were hard-working, hard-drinking men with the gift of the gab, a mixture that won them many friends. There is hardly a town in Britain today without an Irish pub, and around six million British residents have at least one Irish grandparent.

- The influence of Asian immigrants was most famously felt in the food they introduced, with curry practically replacing fish and chips as Britain's 'national dish'. They also brought entrepreneurial spirit on an unprecedented scale, from families running corner shops to skilled scientists and technicians.

- In recent years, net immigration has risen as high as 330,000, not least because of the EU's free movement of labour provision. The largest foreign-born group in the UK is currently Polish, perhaps not surprising given their historic ties with Britain (200,000 Poles were resettled in Britain after the war, including many RAF fighters who helped win the Battle of Britain).

Life-changing stuff

We like to complain about our lot – it's the British way –
but our ancestors in post-war Britain could hardly have
imagined the improvements that were to take place
to provide a better quality of life for Britons alive in
the twenty-first century:

The National Health
Service was introduced
in 1948 with the objective
of providing free healthcare
to all, irrespective of
ability to pay.

The post-war population
explosion required more
houses for people to live in
and more roads for people to
drive on, so more and more
countryside was given over to
satisfying those needs in the
decades that followed.

In the 1970s
people woke up to the
widespread environmental
damage being caused by
unrestricted infrastructure
development, so that the tide of
development today is controlled
to a large extent by planning
regulations and, where
necessary, public
enquiries.

Social stigmas started to crash in the free-loving 1960s, when abortion and homosexuality were both legalised. Equal rights for women got a double boost with the 1970 Equal Pay Act and the 1975 Sex Discrimination Act.

With churches increasingly struggling to fill their pews and trade unions worrying over workers' rights, a rearguard action was fought from the 1970s onwards to prevent shops from opening on a Sunday. Consumerism finally triumphed with the Sunday Trading Act in 1994.

In 2006/07 the UK introduced a permanent smoking ban in public places, instantly improving the quality of life for non-smokers and having an instant impact on the overall well-being of the nation.

Even shops that keep long weekday hours and trade to the maximum on a Sunday can find themselves struggling today in the face of 24/7 online shopping and rapid home delivery (which really kicked off with Amazon in 1995), which is why superstores in particular now provide both in-store and online offerings.

Social media networks continue to grow at a phenomenal pace. Of the (roughly) 60 million people currently above the age of ten in the UK, around 30 million are active Facebook users and around 15–20 million are active users of Twitter, Pinterest, Instagram and/or LinkedIn.

UK population breakdown

The combined population of the UK at the time of the 2011 Census was just over 63 million (32 million female; 31 million male), up from just over 59 million in 2001. Here is the breakdown by individual nation:

BREAKDOWN OF THE UK POPULATION
(AT 2011 CENSUS)

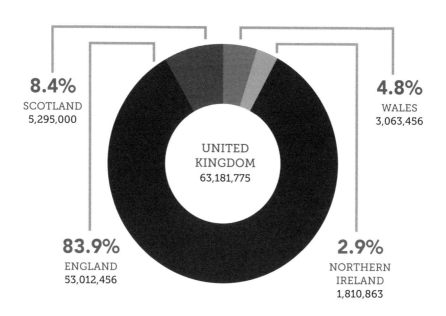

8.4%
SCOTLAND
5,295,000

4.8%
WALES
3,063,456

UNITED
KINGDOM
63,181,775

83.9%
ENGLAND
53,012,456

2.9%
NORTHERN
IRELAND
1,810,863

Note: by 2016 the UK population was estimated by the Office for National Statistics to have risen to around 66 million.

UK POPULATION TRENDS

Although a separate census is held in Scotland and in Northern Ireland, we can detect the following population trends from the 2011 Census held across England and Wales, as this accounted for 84 per cent of the UK population. Where appropriate, 2001 figures are shown in parentheses:

Most people recorded their ethnic background as one of the following:

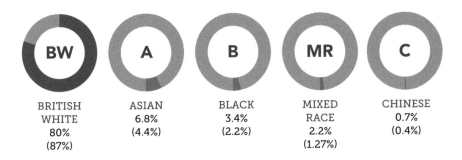

| BRITISH WHITE 80% (87%) | ASIAN 6.8% (4.4%) | BLACK 3.4% (2.2%) | MIXED RACE 2.2% (1.27%) | CHINESE 0.7% (0.4%) |

12% people with partners of a different ethnic group

59% (72) Christian

240,000 people claimed 'other religion', including 176,632 Jedi Knights

7.4% non-UK passport holders

81% 'in good or very good health'

13% born outside the UK

25% (15) no religion

5% (3) Muslim

16% aged 65 or over

7% population rise since 2001

65% (69) homeowners

46.6% (50.9) married

Troubles at home and abroad

The post-war years saw Britain struggle to come to terms with its diminished role in the world. Although it still had a seat at the top table as a founder member of the United Nations (UN) and the North Atlantic Treaty Organization (NATO), it was soon obvious that the new superpowers on the block were the USA and the USSR.

1947: Britain lost the jewel in its imperial crown when it conceded the independence so long demanded by India. The handover was made all the more difficult by the Muslim separatist movement that resulted in the bloody partition into India and Pakistan.

1950–53: As a member of NATO, Britain sent a contingent of troops to support South Korea in the Korean War against Communist-influenced North Korea. It ended in a stalemate that continues to this day.

1956: Britain's diminishing influence in the world was clear to see after it had its knuckles rapped by the UN and the USA for invading Egypt in order to maintain control over the Suez Canal.

1968–98: The Troubles in Northern Ireland ran for 30 years, the main issue being whether the country should remain part of the UK or join the Irish Republic. It ultimately resulted in a power-sharing self-government within the Northern Ireland Assembly.

1981: Inner-city riots occurred in Brixton, London and Toxteth, Liverpool. They were a reaction to the injustices of inner-city life, which are now being tackled at least to an extent with regeneration programmes up and down the country.

1982: Britain retook the Falkland Islands in the South Atlantic within ten weeks of an Argentinian invasion. The issue has not gone away, as Argentina continues to lay claim to the territory they know as Las Malvinas (the Lost Islands).

1991: The break-up of the Soviet Union finally brought an end to the Cold War that had seen the British Secret Intelligence Service and the CIA pit their espionage wits against the KGB of the Soviet Union and the Stasi of East Germany as the world teetered on the brink of World War Three.

1990–91: Britain sent troops to join the Coalition Forces led by the USA in the Gulf War after Kuwait had been invaded by Iraq. Kuwait was liberated and the UN imposed long-term sanctions on Iraq.

1997: The transfer of sovereignty over Hong Kong back to China marked the end of British rule there and was viewed by many historians as the end point of the British Empire.

2003–11: Britain again jumped in with a US-led invasion of Iraq, which resulted in the execution of former dictator Saddam Hussein in 2006 and an eight-year occupation of the country.

Politics

Since the Labour Party under Clement Attlee came to power in 1945, the seesaw politics of Britain have seen Labour and Conservative swap power on a regular basis.

1945–51: The Labour government under Attlee created the welfare state of free education and healthcare, old-age pensions and sickness and unemployment benefits. It also nationalised the Bank of England, the coal and steel industries, the railways and the public utilities.

1951–64: The Conservatives presided over a relatively stable period under Winston Churchill, Anthony Eden, Harold Macmillan and Alec Douglas-Home, although inept handling of the Suez Crisis did cost Anthony Eden his job.

1964–70: Labour under Harold Wilson introduced much social reform, including the relaxation of divorce laws, the banning of capital punishment, the lowering of the voting age to 18 and the establishment of the Open University.

1970–74: The Conservatives under Edward Heath oversaw decimalisation of the British currency in 1971 and entry into the European Economic Community in 1973. They introduced the Three-Day Week in 1974 to conserve electricity during a miners' strike but ironically lost power in that year's general election.

1974–79: Labour back in but Harold Wilson ran out of steam and resigned in 1976. Incoming prime minister James Callaghan was forced into the Lib–Lab pact to hold on to power but the miners' strikes over the Winter of Discontent (1978–79) became his undoing in any event.

1979–97: The Conservatives under Margaret Thatcher, Britain's first female prime minister, presided over the Falklands War, reprivatised many of the nationalised industries and beat the trade unions into submission before being undone by an unpopular poll tax.

John Major took over after a leadership contest in 1990, but rising unemployment, a deep recession and too much squabbling and scandal within the ranks ultimately handed power back to Labour.

1997–2010: Labour enjoyed a long spell from 1997 to 2010 under Tony Blair and, from 2007 onwards, Gordon Brown. Blair presided over the devolution of political power to Scotland, Wales and Northern Ireland, and the introduction of the national minimum wage and the Freedom of Information Act. He ultimately fell from grace over his controversial decision to go to war with Iraq.

2010–: The Conservatives under David Cameron regained power by forming a coalition with the Liberal Democrats. After securing a majority government in 2015, Cameron committed political suicide by calling a referendum on Britain's EU membership in 2016. The result took him by surprise and left his replacement, Theresa May, to negotiate Britain's exit.

THE ROYAL FAMILY

Because King George VI and Queen Elizabeth (the Queen Mother) refused to leave London throughout the Blitz, the Royal Family had regained some popularity following the shame of Edward VIII's abdication in 1936. However, it faced a struggle to reinvent itself in the modern world and a number of high-profile scandals and divorces would not help the cause.

The ups and downs of being royal

A 25-year-old Princess Elizabeth acceded to the throne in 1952, hearing the news of her father's death while in Kenya with the Duke of Edinburgh. She was crowned on 2 June 1953.

The Queen and the Duke of Edinburgh had four children over a 16-year period: Charles (1948), Anne (1950), Andrew (1960) and Edward (1964).

In 1977 the Queen celebrated her Silver Jubilee with a nationwide tour and a number of visits to Commonwealth countries.

The Queen described 1992 as her *annus horribilis* owing to the following events:

- The public rift between Prince Charles and Princess Diana, highlighted by a tell-all biography of Diana.

- The separation of Prince Andrew and Sarah Ferguson, plus topless photographs of her kissing another man.

- The divorce of Princess Anne and Mark Phillips.

- The fire that devastated seven state apartments at Windsor Castle.

The country mourned like never before when Princess Diana was killed in a car crash in Paris in 1997, but the Queen drew criticism because she was slow to react to the news and stayed on a bit too long at Balmoral.

Over a million people lined the streets of London on 6 September 1997 to watch Princess Diana's funeral cortege proceed from Kensington Palace to Westminster Abbey, while 32 million watched on television worldwide.

The Queen's Diamond Jubilee was celebrated across the Commonwealth in 2012 and reached a peak in June with street parties across Britain, an extensive river pageant on the Thames and a huge concert outside Buckingham Palace.

Her Majesty finally became 'cool' when she appeared on film alongside Daniel Craig (as 007 James Bond) during the opening ceremony of the London 2012 Olympic Games, culminating in her arrival in the Olympic Park by parachute (although some claim the jump was made by a double).

Elizabeth II became the longest-ever reigning British monarch on 9 September 2015, finally overtaking her great-great-grandmother Queen Victoria after 63 years, 7 months and 3 days on the throne.

CHAPTER 3

LANDMARKS AND FAMOUS BUILDINGS

Each generation seems to feel the need to mark its territory on a grand scale, to leave its historical footprint behind to be admired by future generations. This often takes the form of a magnificent building or striking monument, sometimes erected to provide a functional purpose, sometimes built just to make a statement. At other times, though, a landmark just turns up as a result of nature doing its own thing, which is where we're going to start.

Nelson's
Column

Natural landmarks

From the White Cliffs of Dover to the Giant's Causeway of County Antrim, Mother Nature has provided inspiring landmarks throughout history without even trying. Sometimes mankind provides a helping hand, though, by carving into the natural canvas provided.

DAN-YR-OGOF CAVES, WALES

Often voted Britain's greatest natural wonder, the vast cave network carved by water deep within the Brecon Beacons is breathtaking. The highlights include rock formations known as Angel, Alabaster Pillar and Rasher of Bacon.

GIANT'S CAUSEWAY, NORTHERN IRELAND

The Giant's Causeway consists of around 40,000 hexagonal basalt columns rising out of the sea. Its geometric nature results from the way lava cools after a volcanic eruption, but its name derives from folklore about a giant named Finn MacCool, who built the columns as stepping stones in order to fight a rival Scottish giant across the water.

FINGAL'S CAVE, SCOTLAND

The cathedral-like structure of the sea cave here gives rise to wonderful acoustics and resulted in Felix Mendelssohn immortalising the wonder in his acclaimed overture *The Hebrides*. Its natural beauty was captured by Romantic painter J. M. W. Turner in his painting *Staffa, Fingal's Cave*.

JURASSIC COAST, DEVON AND DORSET

The important geology of the so-called Jurassic Coast in fact spans the Triassic, Jurassic and Cretaceous periods of pre-history, providing a time capsule of 185 million years of plant and animal fossils, including those of the extinct Pterosaur (winged lizard) and Ichthyosaur (fish lizard). The natural wonders of the 96-mile coastline include Lyme Bay, Lulworth Cove, Chesil Beach, Durdle Door and the Isle of Portland.

THE WHITE CLIFFS OF DOVER, KENT

Presiding over the narrowest part of the English Channel, the White Cliffs of Dover are as striking as they are strategically important. Immortalised in the eponymous 1942 Vera Lynn hit song, the bluebirds within the lyrics refer to the blue uniforms of the RAF fighter pilots who had won the Battle of Britain above the cliffs in 1940.

CERNE ABBAS GIANT, DORSET

The Cerne Abbas Giant is a 55-metre-tall club-wielding figure carved into a chalk hillside, probably created in the seventeenth century as a fertility symbol. Folklore had it that fertility could be obtained by 'coupling' within the outline of the giant's erect penis, but I should warn you that it is today a popular tourist attraction should you feel so inclined.

Castles, palaces and stately homes

Britain is positively spoiled for magnificent castles, originally built throughout the land for defensive purposes, and royal palaces and stately homes, built to keep monarchs and nobles in the style to which they had long since become accustomed and to allow them to entertain on a grand scale. They capture much of our history within their walls.

WINDSOR CASTLE, BERKSHIRE

Knocked up as a wooden hilltop fort by William the Conqueror, successive monarchs made improvements that resulted in State Apartments stuffed full of art and other treasures. St George's Chapel is the resting place of Henry VIII and his favourite wife Jane Seymour, as well as Charles I, who was buried there after having his head sewn back on. A devastating fire in 1992 laid waste to a hundred rooms but they were quickly restored to their former glory.

HAMPTON COURT PALACE, LONDON

Henry VIII's Tudor home was greatly improved by William III in the seventeenth century in an attempt to rival the Palace of Versailles. Go there to admire the famous maze, the historic real tennis court, the Tudor kitchens and the art of the Royal Collection, including works by Canaletto and Rembrandt.

SANDRINGHAM HOUSE, NORFOLK

Sandringham House was bought in 1862 for the Prince of Wales (the future Edward VII) and his wife, Princess Alexandra of Denmark, who was keen to live there because the scenery and climate reminded her of her home across the North Sea. It is still used by the Royal Family today as a country retreat.

BUCKINGHAM PALACE, LONDON

Known to the Royal Family as Buck House, Buckingham Palace started life as an eighteenth-century townhouse. It became the London home of the monarch when Queen Victoria took up residence in 1837. The Queen Mother was famously pleased when a German bomb destroyed the chapel during the Blitz, because she felt that she could at least then 'look the East End in the face'.

AN ESTATE AGENT'S VIEW OF BUCKINGHAM PALACE

- Price on request
- 77,000 sq m
- Three wings around central courtyard
- 'Private' balcony on principal façade
- Exceptional views of St James's Park and Admiralty Arch
- Well placed for national rejoicing and mourning
- 775 rooms in total, including 52 principal bedrooms
- 19 State Rooms for entertaining family and friends
- Music Room, flanked by Blue and White Drawing Rooms

- Ample accommodation for servants
- Largest private garden in London (40 acres), with lake, helicopter landing area and tennis court
- Adjacent mews, with Gold State Coach and horses (subject to separate negotiation)
- Picture Gallery with priceless art collection (also subject to separate negotiation)
- Belle Époque cream and gold interior
- Exceptionally well maintained by present owners
- Viewing recommended

BLENHEIM PALACE, OXFORDSHIRE

The English Baroque-style Blenheim Palace was gifted by Queen Anne to John Churchill, the 1st Duke of Marlborough, after he led Allied forces to victory against the French at the Battle of Blenheim in 1704. It has been owned by successive Dukes of Marlborough ever since.

EDINBURGH CASTLE, SCOTLAND

Edinburgh Castle rises spectacularly out of the volcanic rock above Princes Street Gardens. Given its history as a place of battle – it is one of the most besieged castles in history – it is the perfect venue for the annual Edinburgh Military Tattoo and the National War Museum of Scotland.

BALMORAL CASTLE, SCOTLAND

The Royal Family's Scottish holiday home in Royal Deeside was completed in the Scots Baronial style in 1856 for Queen Victoria's husband, Prince Albert, and was the setting for Victoria's peculiar relationship with the ghillie John Brown during her long period of mourning following Albert's death. It commands fine views of the Dee river valley and contains seven Munros (mountains over 3,000 ft) within its grounds.

CAERNARFON CASTLE, WALES

Caernarfon Castle was one of many stone strongholds built by Edward I to keep his Welsh subjects in check in the thirteenth century. Edward's son (Edward II) was born in the castle in 1284 and it has twice hosted the investiture of the Prince of Wales: the future Edward VIII in 1911 and Prince Charles in 1969.

CARRICKFERGUS CASTLE, NORTHERN IRELAND

Built in 1177, Carrickfergus Castle at the top of Belfast Lough saw action in 1210 when put under siege by King John, in 1597 during the Nine Years' War (a rebellion against English rule), in 1760 when invaded by the French and in 1778 when a naval battle of the American Revolutionary War was fought in the waters below.

Other iconic British buildings

Some iconic buildings started life as mere designs to fulfil a particular purpose, whether commercial, political, religious, educational or cultural, but we can tell with the benefit of hindsight that their unique design and structure had them destined for historical greatness from the start.

Westminster Abbey, London

The Gothic-style Westminster Abbey has been the scene of coronations and 16 royal weddings since 1066. It is also the final resting place of 17 monarchs and, in Poets' Corner, many great British writers, including Geoffrey Chaucer, Samuel Johnson, Charles Dickens, Alfred Tennyson, Thomas Hardy and Rudyard Kipling.

10 Downing Street, London

In 1735, Number 10 Downing Street was offered by George II as a personal gift to William Walpole, Britain's first prime minister, but Walpole accepted it only as an official residence and temporary home for himself and future prime ministers.

Palace of Westminster, London

The Palace of Westminster, also known as the Houses of Parliament because it includes the House of Lords and House of Commons, was completed in the Perpendicular Gothic Revival style in 1870, having been largely rebuilt after a fire destroyed the original in 1834.

A TOUR OF THE HOUSES OF PARLIAMENT

Westminster Hall: one of the remaining medieval sections of the palace, it was the largest hall in Europe when it was originally built in 1097.

Chapel of St Mary Undercroft: one of the few remaining medieval parts of the building. Suffragette Emily Davison hid in a cupboard in the chapel the night before the 1911 census so that her address would be recorded as the House of Commons.

House of Lords Chamber: setting for the State Opening of Parliament by the reigning monarch. Commons members are allowed to watch from the door but are not allowed in.

Central Lobby: the octagonal crossroads of the palace, situated between the House of Commons and the House of Lords.

Victoria Tower: this contains the archives of the House of Commons and the House of Lords.

Elizabeth Tower: arguably London's best-known landmark, it is more commonly known as Big Ben, which is in fact the name of the tower's main bell.

House of Commons Chamber: had to be rebuilt after being bombed during World War Two. The two red lines separating the government benches from the opposition benches are just over two sword-lengths apart.

Royal Pavilion, Brighton, East Sussex

The Royal Pavilion was completed in 1823 as a seaside retreat for the Prince Regent, the future George IV, because he needed somewhere to spend dirty weekends away with Maria Fitzherbert, the Catholic woman he had secretly (and unlawfully) married in 1785. The exterior was built in the Indo-Islamic style, complete with domes and minarets, and the interior reflects the Chinese, Mughal and Islamic influences of the time.

Stormont Parliament Buildings, Northern Ireland

The Stormont Parliament Buildings in Belfast were built in the Greek classical style with white Portland stone to house the separate parliament building needed for Northern Ireland following partition in 1922. The first time it served a non-political use was to accommodate the many people who wanted to attend the funeral of footballer George Best in 2005.

St Paul's Cathedral, London

After it burned down in the Great Fire of London in 1666, Christopher Wren designed the current English Baroque version of St Paul's Cathedral. It was again repaired after being bombed during World War Two. It has played host to the funerals of Horatio Nelson, the Duke of Wellington, Winston Churchill and Margaret Thatcher, as well as the wedding of Prince Charles and Lady Diana.

Rosslyn Chapel, Scotland

The towering sixteenth-century Rosslyn Chapel in Roslin, Midlothian is considered to have connections to the Knights Templar and the Holy Grail, earning it a starring role in Dan Brown's 2003 novel *The Da Vinci Code* and its 2006 film adaptation.

Tintern Abbey, Wales

Founded in 1131 and developed over the following 400 years, the Cistercian Tintern Abbey fell victim to Henry VIII's Dissolution of the Monasteries in the sixteenth century. Its substantial Gothic ruins have been commemorated in art and poetry ever since and even today remain an impressive sight.

Superstructures

Whether monuments and other awe-inspiring structures get built for a practical purpose, or to provide pleasure, or to make a statement of love, devotion or admiration, they somehow end up defining a nation every bit as much as its famous buildings and natural landmarks. Britain is no exception.

AVEBURY AND STONEHENGE, WILTSHIRE

The 47 stones of Stonehenge on Salisbury Plain are the more famous of these Neolithic monuments used thousands of years ago for pagan rituals, but the 76 stones in the circles at Avebury spread themselves wider and you can wander all over the site for free.

BLACKPOOL TOWER, LANCASHIRE

Opened in 1894, the Blackpool Tower emulated the style of the Eiffel Tower in Paris, which had opened just five years earlier. It contains one of the grandest rooms in the country, the Tower Ballroom, which is used as a venue for certain episodes of the BBC's popular *Strictly Come Dancing* programme.

THE EDEN PROJECT, CORNWALL

The Eden Project in Cornwall, completed in 2000, is a magnificent example of how to transform an ugly industrial blot on the landscape (in this case, disused china clay pits) into a first-class tourist attraction. The extreme environments of planet earth, from humid rainforest to dry desert, are replicated within its huge domes, which themselves look as if they have been lifted straight from a science-fiction movie.

SAMSON AND GOLIATH, NORTHERN IRELAND

The two iconic canary-yellow shipbuilding cranes that loom over Belfast stand in the shipyard of Harland and Wolff. They are not quite identical, as

Goliath (completed in 1969) stands at 96 m and Samson (completed in 1974) is slightly taller at 106 m. Although shipbuilding at the yard has ceased, the cranes are still used for ship repairs and structural engineering and offshore construction projects.

ANGEL OF THE NORTH, TYNE AND WEAR

Completed in 1998, Antony Gormley's contemporary steel structure the *Angel of the North* transforms the landscape around it and seems to provide a friendly welcome to all who pass below on the A1 road or the East Coast Main Line railway. It stands 20 m tall and has a wingspan of 54 m, almost the equivalent of a jumbo jet.

FORTH BRIDGE, SCOTLAND

The Forth Bridge is the iconic symbol of Scotland immortalised in the 1935 Hitchcock film *The 39 Steps* (based on the 1915 John Buchan novel). Completed in 1890 to carry trains across the river west of Edinburgh, it was Britain's first all-steel bridge, but it has always had the appearance of iron owing to the red oxide paint used to preserve it.

HADRIAN'S WALL, NORTHUMBERLAND AND CUMBRIA

Hadrian's Wall was so well built by the Romans 2,000 years ago to keep out the marauding Picts of present-day Scotland that many parts remain visible alongside its 73-mile length from the North Sea in the east to the Solway Firth in the west.

PONTCYSYLLTE AQUEDUCT, WALES

Designed by Thomas Telford, the magnificent Pontcysyllte Aqueduct in Wrexham is the highest and longest in Britain. It was built in cast iron on top of stone pillars in 1805, the same year as the Battle of Trafalgar, and it still fulfils its original purpose of carrying narrowboats and walkers along the Llangollen Canal 38 m above the River Dee.

NELSON'S COLUMN, LONDON

Towering above Trafalgar Square, Nelson's Column was completed in 1843 to recognise the naval achievements of Admiral Horatio Nelson. Let's take a closer look at it.

Capital (the bit at the top of the column just below Lord Nelson):

- Consists of bronze acanthus leaves and scrolls
- Made with melted-down cannon from HMS *Royal George*
- Based on Temple of Mars Ultor in Rome

Statue of Lord Nelson:

- 5.5 m high
- Made of Craigleith sandstone
- Designed by Edwin Landseer
- Sculpted by Edward Hodges Baily
- Got a chipped shoulder when struck by lightning in 1896

Column:

- Made of Dartmoor granite
- Corinthian style, i.e. fluted

Whole monument:

- 51.6 m high
- Weighs 2,500 tons
- Cost £47,000 (around £4 million in today's money)
- Private investors included the Tsar of Russia
- Overall design by William Railton

Pedestal:

- Four bronze panels added between 1849 and 1854
- Panels were cast from captured French guns
- Panels portray the Battle of Cape St Vincent (1797), the Battle of the Nile (1798), the Battle of Copenhagen (1801) and the Battle of Trafalgar (1805)

Four lions:

- Added in 1867
- Designed by Edwin Landseer

CHAPTER 4

GREAT BRITONS

There can be no doubt that Britain has produced more than its fair share of inventions, cures, breakthroughs and discoveries. From seafaring Francis Drake to astronaut Tim Peake, it seems that Britons have never been able to get enough of learning more about other lives and worlds. From Isaac Newton to Tim Berners-Lee, the genius of many Britons has played a large part in the way in which people live their lives around the world. From Florence Nightingale to Professor Frank Pantridge, some Britons have never tired of caring about their fellow humans.

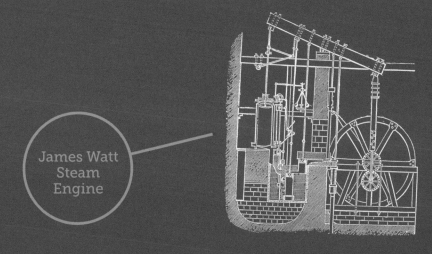

James Watt
Steam
Engine

Great British explorers

A great number of British men and women have taken it upon themselves to explore the far-flung corners of the earth in order to find fame or advance their own particular causes. Here are just a few of their awe-inspiring stories.

FRANCIS DRAKE (1540–96)

The most famous explorer of the Elizabethan age, Francis Drake became wealthy as a pirate and slave trader before being sponsored by Elizabeth I to circumnavigate the globe in the *Golden Hind* (1577–80). He was instrumental in the defeat of the Spanish Armada in 1588.

WALTER RALEIGH (1552–1618)

Walter Raleigh travelled to the New World, establishing the colony of Virginia and famously bringing back the potato and tobacco. He was forever overstepping the mark with unsanctioned excessive force against the Spanish, which ultimately led to his execution.

CAPTAIN JAMES COOK (1728–79)

James Cook was the first explorer to cross the Antarctic Circle, claimed New South Wales in Australia for Britain, circumnavigated New Zealand for the first time, and mapped out the Hawaiian Islands. He was stabbed to death by unfriendly natives on Hawaii.

LADY HESTER STANHOPE (1776–1839)

Often disguised as a man, carrying a sword and riding an Arab stallion, the self-styled Queen of the Desert was the first explorer to carry out archaeological research in the Holy Land.

DAVID LIVINGSTONE (1813–73)

After surviving a lion attack in 1840 with just a broken arm, medical missionary and anti-slavery campaigner David Livingstone went on to become the first explorer to cross Southern Africa from west to east after discovering the source of the Zambezi River.

MARY KINGSLEY (1862–1900)

Mary Kingsley took herself off to the uncharted parts of West Africa at the age of 30. She wrote against European imperialism, championed the rights of the indigenous people and collected fish species on behalf of the British Museum.

ROBERT FALCON SCOTT (1868–1912)

Robert Scott was a captain in the Royal Navy who first discovered the Polar Plateau on which the South Pole is situated. He became the first British explorer to reach the South Pole in 1912 (having been pipped at the post by Norway's Roald Amundsen to be the first ever explorer to reach it), but sadly never returned from the ill-fated trip.

RANULPH FIENNES (1944–)

Widely recognised as the world's greatest living explorer, ex-army officer Ranulph Fiennes led the first expedition to circumnavigate the globe on its polar axis using only surface transport and he climbed Mount Everest at the age of 65.

TIM PEAKE (1972–)

Ex-army helicopter pilot Tim Peake undertook a six-month mission to the International Space Station in 2015–16 after intensive training as an astronaut. While there, he became the first British astronaut to complete a spacewalk.

Great British inventors

British inventors have consistently come up with the means to improve the quality of life for millions of people around the world. Here is but a small collection of their achievements.

JOHN HARRISON (1693–1776)

John Harrison was a clockmaker who solved the problem of identifying longitude at sea. Using Harrison's H4 marine chronometer, ocean-going ships were less likely to miss their destination and flounder on uncharted rocks.

JOSEPH FRY (1728–87)

Joseph Fry came up with a method to grind cocoa beans using a Watt steam engine, which in turn led to the Fry's Chocolate Cream bar (1866), Britain's first chocolate Easter egg (1873) and the Fry's Turkish Delight (1914).

THOMAS WEDGWOOD (1771–1805)

Son of the industrial potter Josiah Wedgwood, Thomas Wedgwood is credited with producing the first ever image taken by a camera, using cloth and white leather coated with silver nitrate exposed to natural sunlight.

JOSEPH SWAN (1828–1914)

Joseph Swan created the incandescent light bulb in 1880 and his house in Gateshead was the first in the world to be so lit. The ships of the Royal Navy would be amongst the early beneficiaries of his invention.

ALEXANDER GRAHAM BELL (1847–1922)

Driven by his desire to teach speech to the deaf, Alexander Graham Bell experimented with the conversion of electricity into sound and with the idea of transmitting speech through a receiver. In 1876 he was granted a US patent for the telephone.

JOHN LOGIE BAIRD (1888–1946)

John Logie Baird developed the first working television in 1926 and went on to invent the colour television and the first electronic picture tube. His company was behind the first BBC television programme.

ALAN TURING (1912–54)

Mathematician Alan Turing invented the electric computer even before he set about breaking the German Enigma code during the Second World War, which is said to have shortened the war by several years and thereby saved millions of lives.

JAMES DYSON (1947–)

James Dyson launched his revolutionary bagless vacuum cleaner in 1983. Undeterred by initial resistance from distributors who wanted to maintain the status quo, he launched it in Japan (where it won awards) and the USA, and eventually in Britain in 1993.

TIM BERNERS-LEE (1955–)

Computer scientist Tim Berners-Lee was a keen trainspotter as a child and picked up a basic knowledge of electronics through tinkering with his model railway. It was, of course, only a small jump from tinkering with a model railway to inventing the World Wide Web in 1989.

Great British engineers

The genius of British engineers down the centuries is such that many of their achievements remain standing and in use today, or provided the prototypes for the rest of the world to develop their own infrastructures.

JAMES WATT (1736–1819)

James Watt has become a household name because the measurement of electrical and mechanical power is named in his honour, as in 100-watt light bulb, 10-kilowatt battery. He improved the steam engine in the 1770s to the extent that it revolutionised the efficiency of industry.

POSSIBLE SALES PITCH FOR A JAMES WATT STEAM ENGINE IN 1800

- Reliable 5–10 horsepower on all products
- Over a thousand satisfied customers right across British industry
- 308 mill-powering machines and 190 pumps sold to date
- Separate steam condenser chamber allows you to use 75 per cent less coal to power your new engine
- Leave your watermill to the vagaries of the inconstant river and build your factory in the city
- Available with portable frame for on-site construction
- Pump-driven water extraction allows you to mine for tin and coal without getting your feet soaked
- Don't rely on sail – reduce the time of your passengers' journeys on a steam-powered ship
- Maintain power throughout your spinning process to create quality cloth with no wastage

THOMAS TELFORD (1757–1834)

Dubbed the Colossus of Roads, Thomas Telford was a prolific builder of highways, bridges, harbours and canals, including the Ellesmere Canal, the Caledonian Canal through the Scottish Highlands and the Menai Suspension Bridge.

RICHARD TREVITHICK (1771–1833)

Engineer Richard Trevithick developed the first high-pressure steam engine for mining use in 1802 and the first railway steam locomotive in 1804, paving the way for others to develop working locomotives to haul coal and then passengers.

GEORGE STEPHENSON (1781–1848)

Initially ridiculed for the very idea of it, George Stephenson completed the Liverpool to Manchester Railway in 1830, the first public railway line to run between two cities anywhere in the world.

ISAMBARD KINGDOM BRUNEL (1806–59)

Brunel's amazing achievements included dockyards, transatlantic steamships like the SS *Great Britain*, the Clifton Suspension Bridge and the Great Western Railway, including revolutionary viaducts and the two-mile-long Box Tunnel.

FRANK WHITTLE (1907–96)

In the 1930s and 1940s, after he left the Royal Air Force, Air Commodore Frank Whittle developed the first jet engine so that aircraft could fly higher to achieve faster speeds and longer distances. By the 1950s jet-engined aircraft were under production worldwide on a commercial basis.

Great British pioneers of medicine

From vaccination to portable defibrillation, the achievements of British medical pioneers continue to save countless lives and improve the quality of life for many others around the world.

EDWARD JENNER (1749–1823)

In the 1790s, to the horror of the medical establishment and the press, Edward Jenner inoculated children with pus from diseased cows and went on to prove that this prevented the children from contracting the dreaded smallpox.

JOHN SNOW (1813–58)

John Snow proved in 1850 that an outbreak of cholera in London had been caused by unclean water from a public pump, resulting in fundamental changes to the provision of water and waste removal in London and other cities around the world.

FLORENCE NIGHTINGALE (1820–1910)

Hailed as the founder of modern nursing, Florence Nightingale proved during the Crimean War (1853–1856) that trained nurses and clean hospitals substantially reduced the rate of death from infection.

THE SITUATION WHEN FLORENCE NIGHTINGALE ARRIVED IN THE CRIMEA

37
nurses

18,000
dying and wounded

300 miles
miles between battlefield and hospital across the Black Sea

✚ Miles of hospital corridors piled up with bodies

✚ Rampant cholera and lice

✚ Blood-clotted bandages

✚ Watery soup as sole food source for patients

THE MOTHER OF INFOGRAPHICS

Florence Nightingale didn't just pioneer medical care, she also pioneered infographics. She used bar charts, pie charts and her famous coxcomb (or 'rose diagram') to alert the powers that be, including Parliament and Queen Victoria, to the main causes of death in the Crimea.

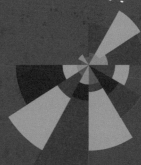

JOSEPH LISTER
(1827–1912)

Known as the 'father of antiseptic surgery', surgeon Joseph Lister shared Florence Nightingale's obsession with cleanliness and determined that post-operative wounds had to be properly cleaned and covered to prevent infection and the spread of airborne disease.

ALEXANDER FLEMING
(1881–1955)

Having served in the Royal Army Medical Corps during World War One, Alexander Fleming returned to his medical research and, in 1928, discovered penicillin while studying influenza. In 1945 Fleming received the Nobel Prize for Medicine.

PROFESSOR FRANK PANTRIDGE (1916–2004)

After being awarded the Military Cross for gallantry during World War Two, cardiologist Frank Pantridge went on to introduce the modern cardiopulmonary resuscitation system and revolutionised paramedic services with specially adapted ambulances and the portable defibrillator.

Great British scientists

From the laws of motion to the Big Bang theory, British scientists have never shied away from the big questions and the world is a better and more understood place for their hard work and determination.

ISAAC NEWTON (1642–1726)

English physicist and mathematician Isaac Newton didn't just discover that apples fell from trees through the force of gravity, he also came up with the laws of motion, the first practical telescope, and the first coins to be designed and produced with anti-counterfeit measures.

MICHAEL FARADAY (1791–1867)

Michael Faraday's discoveries in the fields of electricity, magnetism, optics and gases resulted in many practical innovations and improvements to lighthouses, electric power and refrigeration.

CHARLES DARWIN (1809–82)

Naturalist Charles Darwin changed the way humans viewed themselves forever. His work on evolution and natural selection, bolstered by his findings on the Galapagos Islands in 1835, overturned the long-held view that all life was as it was because that was how it had been created.

DOROTHY HODGKIN (1910–94)

Biochemist Dorothy Hodgkin helped discover the structure of proteins, including those relating to penicillin and vitamin B12, and insulin, which was important to the understanding and treatment of diabetes. She won the Nobel Prize for Chemistry in 1964.

FRANCIS CRICK (1916–2004)

Francis Crick, working with American James Watson and drawing on the research findings of two other British scientists, Maurice Wilkins and Rosalind Franklin, published the structure of DNA in 1953.

STEPHEN HAWKING (1942–)

Stephen Hawking is renowned for explaining difficult concepts in understandable ways, and his work on black holes helped confirm the Big Bang theory, because black holes are a bit like the Big Bang in reverse. He has achieved a huge amount in spite of the motor neurone disease that has afflicted him since the age of 21.

380,000 years: time it took for matter to cool sufficiently for atoms to be formed

5.9 billion years: time it took for our solar system to be born

3 minutes: time it took for light chemicals to be created

BIG BANG THEORY

13.8 billion years ago: when the Big Bang occurred

5 billion years: time left before our sun burns itself out

80 billion: galaxies created as the ultimate result of the Big Bang

10 billion °F: temperature in the first second of the universe's life

CHAPTER 5

BRITISH FASHION

From strict period costume to the anything-goes era of individual style, British designers have never let up in their efforts to satisfy the demands of each generation's dedicated followers of fashion.

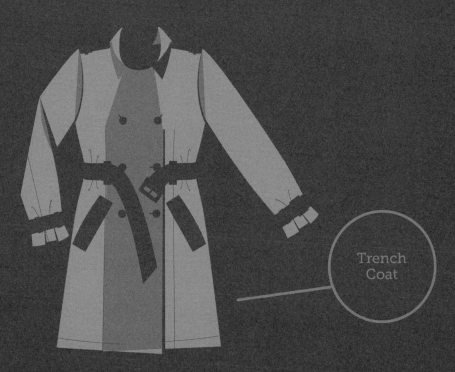

Trench Coat

British clothing through the ages

ELIZABETHAN FASHION

British fashion really took off in the Elizabethan era when breeches and hosiery (think Walter Raleigh), and structured dresses over corsets and drum-shaped farthingales (think Elizabeth I) finally replaced the tunics and pointed shoes of earlier times.

GEORGIAN/REGENCY FASHION

The Georgian/Regency fashion of the eighteenth and early nineteenth centuries had the men looking dandy in cravats, cut-away coats and riding hats (think Beau Brummell), and the ladies looking full-figured in high-waisted, bosom-lifting, flowing dresses (think Jane Austen).

VICTORIAN FASHION

The Victorian fashion of the nineteenth century had the men looking sober in tailored suits and top hats (think Isambard Kingdom Brunel), and the women completely imprisoned within impractical high-collared, full-length dresses (think Queen Victoria) that had to be worn even while nursing, horse riding or playing tennis.

ROARING TWENTIES

The roaring twenties blew away everything that came before with the ladies sporting shorter, looser flapper dresses, shorter hair and smaller hats. The men wore baggier trousers with two-toned shoes and gangster hats.

WARTIME FASHION

A 'make do and mend' culture prevailed while clothes were rationed along with everything else during the world wars and beyond. Women wore practical daytime clothing that wouldn't get caught up in machinery and made their own dresses. Men wore out the one suit that they had. Even Princess Elizabeth had to collect clothing coupons for her wedding dress in 1947.

Clothes rationing in World War Two

Civilian clothing was rationed from 1941 onwards, starting with 66 coupons per annum for each adult but greatly reducing during the course of the war. The following number of coupons were required for individual items (plus whatever was necessary to make up the cash value).

4 camiknickers

4 men's pants

1 tie

7 men's shoes

16 raincoat or overcoat (14 for women, 11 for a child)

11 dress

8 men's shirt

8 gym tunic (an essential part of a girl's school uniform)

8 trousers

5 women's shoes

2 women's stockings

SWINGING SIXTIES

The Cool Britannia age of the Mary Quant-inspired miniskirt, worn by the more adventurous girls with go-go boots and colourful make-up, saw the men experiment with longer hairstyles, military coats, flower-power shirts, flared and bell-bottomed trousers, and platform shoes. London's Carnaby Street was the place to see and be seen.

HIPPY CHIC AND UNISEX

The 1970s enjoyed the disco age of Laura Ashley-inspired maxi dresses and choker necklaces for the women, and tank tops over big-collared shirts and flares for the men. For those who preferred a more muted approach, there were practical unisex tracksuits, denim jeans and slogan T-shirts.

ANYTHING GOES

Rock, heavy metal and punk styles of music started to influence fashion from the late 1970s, with Vivienne Westwood at the heart of the 'anything goes' revolution. Leather, tartan, spikes, safety pins, Dr. Martens and the Union Jack somehow joined forces to create the 1990s version of the Cool Britannia look.

VINTAGE AND RETRO

As the second half of the twentieth century left few fashion ideas unexplored, the obvious way forward for twenty-first-century designers and followers of fashion became vintage and retro, with each generation demanding their own twists on what had gone before to create a new multibillion worldwide industry.

Iconic British items of clothing

Some British fashion designs refused to go away at the end of the era they originally belonged to, enduring instead for decades or even centuries in some cases. Here are a few such examples of fashions that stood the test of time:

TARTAN: once the everyday garb of the Scottish Highlander as far back as 2,000 years ago, each clan having its own distinctive pattern and colour scheme, today tartan enjoys universal appeal worldwide, being used in pretty much any fashion item made in pretty much any material.

WELLINGTON BOOTS: made popular by the Duke of Wellington in the early nineteenth century, the boots became an outdoor staple of the British aristocracy and prevail to this day as the choice of rubber footwear for music festival goers in Britain.

PAISLEY PATTERN: the Scottish town of Paisley became the world centre for thread-making in the nineteenth century, and exported shawls and other garments in the Paisley pattern all over the world. The teardrop pattern was adopted from one of Persian origin, used for a long time to make Kashmir shawls in the shadow of the Himalayas.

HARRIS TWEED: named after the island of Lewis and Harris in the Outer Hebrides of Scotland, the strength of the handwoven wool was ideal for protection against the cold climate there, but the quality of the fabric means it remains much sought after by couturiers and high-end clothing and accessory retailers around the world.

TRENCH COAT: originally an item of tough, waterproof clothing developed for British Army officers fighting in the trenches, hence the garment's name. Its traditional colour was khaki, but the ones still made today by Burberry and Aquascutum (both of whom claim to have invented the garment) come in a variety of fashionable colours in order to appeal to as wide a market as possible.

SAVILE ROW SUIT: any suit made by a Savile Row tailor in London has been for centuries synonymous with bespoke excellence. Famous customers have included Lord Nelson, Napoleon III, Winston Churchill, Prince Charles and Jude Law.

DEERSTALKER: immortalised by drawings of Arthur Conan Doyle's fictional detective Sherlock Holmes, the deerstalker was popular in the nineteenth century with game hunters and has been popular ever since with hat lovers. The fore and aft caps offer protection against the sun and the flaps on top untie to drop down over the ears whenever a chill wind blows.

BOWLER HAT: originally an alternative to the top hat, which was too easily knocked off by low branches while horse riding, the hard felt bowler hat became synonymous with city gents working in the financial district of London. Its comedy appeal was used to good effect by Charlie Chaplin and Laurel and Hardy.

CHAPTER 6

TRANSPORTING BRITAIN

It was the quality of British shipbuilding that once allowed Britannia to rule the waves. Then we gave trains to the world, designed some of the most beautiful cars ever produced and took to designing and building aircraft like a duck to water. This chapter admires some of the most iconic transport machines we have produced for use on sea and land and in the air.

Aston Martin DB5

Great British ships

It is perhaps not surprising that an island nation should become rather good at building and sailing ships, but Britain used those skills to discover new worlds and win numerous sea battles against fleets far larger than her own.

MARY ROSE

Launched in 1511 and sunk in battle in 1545, the *Mary Rose* was a purpose-built four-storey wooden warship of the Tudor navy of King Henry VIII. She saw action in battles against France, Brittany and Scotland before finally sinking while leading an attack against the French in the Solent. Salvaged in 1982, her remains are on display in Portsmouth Historic Dockyard, alongside many Tudor artefacts found on board.

HMS *ENDEAVOUR*

The Endeavour was the Royal Navy research ship captained by James Cook on his first voyage to Australia and New Zealand (1769–71). She sailed west from Plymouth to round Cape Horn on the way to Tahiti, then crossed uncharted waters of the Pacific Ocean to reach New Zealand and the east coast of Australia, anchoring at Botany Bay. She completed her circumnavigation by rounding the Cape of Good Hope on the way home.

HMS *VICTORY*

Lord Nelson's flagship Victory was one of the largest wooden warships ever built and saw action in the French Revolutionary and Napoleonic Wars. Her finest hour was at the Battle of Trafalgar in 1805, but it was also her saddest hour because Nelson died of his wounds on board that day. Now a museum ship in Portsmouth Historic Dockyard, she is also the current flagship of the First Sea Lord of the Royal Navy, making her the world's oldest naval ship still in commission.

RMS *TITANIC*

The largest ship in the world when she was launched in Belfast, the majestic *Titanic* proved less unsinkable than people thought after striking an iceberg on her maiden voyage in 1912.

THE *TITANIC* IN NUMBERS

2
age in months of Millvina Dean, the youngest Titanic survivor (died 2009, aged 97)

710
number of survivors

24
top speed in knots

3,000
number of workers who built her

700
number of people who managed to get into a lifeboat

16,850
number of bottles of wine, beer and spirits in fully stocked bar

22.5
speed in knots at impact

1,100
capacity of lifeboats

4
number of days at sea before hitting the iceberg

46,000
ship's weight in tons

1,514
number who perished at sea

370
distance in miles from land (Newfoundland) when it sank

160
time in minutes between impact and sinking

60
time in minutes between collision and launch of first lifeboat

2,224
total people on board

1,100
spare capacity on maiden voyage

1,316
number of passengers on board

2,070
distance in miles travelled before hitting the iceberg

908
number of crew members on board

Great British trains

From the steam locomotive that paved the way to a record-breaking diesel engine, Britain gave railways and locomotive engineering to the world. Here are just a few of the iconic trains that should never be forgotten.

ROCKET

Built in 1829, Robert Stephenson's *Rocket* was a distinctive-looking piece of engineering with its tall smokestack chimney and two large front driving wheels. Impressively fast and reliable for its time, it became the template for most steam locomotives around the world for the next 150 years.

KERR, STUART ENGINES

Between 1890 and 1920, Kerr, Stuart and Company exported their tough little tank engines around the world. The tugboats of the railway world, they hauled sugar cane on Antigua, provided supplies to troops during the Second Boer War in South Africa, helped construct the Nile Delta Barrage and supplied coal to the generators of the Admiralty's wireless station in the Falkland Islands.

FLYING SCOTSMAN

The Nigel Gresley-designed *Flying Scotsman* became the first steam locomotive to reach 100 mph in 1934 and still holds the world record for the longest non-stop run by a steam locomotive (422 miles). Retired in 1963, it then made 'farewell tours' to North America and Australia. It is now hauling special train services on British main lines following a ten-year overhaul at the National Railway Museum in York.

MALLARD

Another Nigel Gresley-designed steam locomotive, but *Mallard* had a Bugatti-style streamlined shape to lower wind resistance, which paid off when it broke the world speed record for a steam locomotive in 1938, reaching 125.88 mph near Grantham in Lincolnshire.

London Underground in numbers

270
stations

49,802
distance in miles travelled each year
by the Tube's escalators, i.e. twice
the circumference of the earth

249
miles of track

55
percentage of London
Underground network that
is actually above ground

3
Tube stations that
lie outside the M25
orbital motorway

300
National Gallery
paintings stored
in Aldwych
station during
World War Two

79
number of stations
that installed bunk
beds to sleep
22,000 people
during air raids in
World War Two

10.50
amount in pounds
and pence paid
to Harry Beck for
designing the Tube
map in 1933

11 lines

1 billion plus
journeys made
on the Tube
each year

20
travel time in seconds
between Leicester Square
and Covent Garden
on the Piccadilly line

Great British motors

British cars were known for their quality and design in equal measure and many of them continue to stand out today as sought-after classic cars or design icons.

ROLLS-ROYCE SILVER GHOST

First produced in 1906, the Silver Ghost (so called due to the ghost-like quietness of its engine) was soon declared by *Autocar* magazine to be the best car in the world. The same chassis and engine were used to produce the British Army's armoured cars throughout World War One.

MINI

Made in 1959 to provide an economy car at a time of fuel shortage following the Suez Crisis, the Mini quickly became a British icon, culminating in a starring role in the 1969 film *The Italian Job*. Nimble enough to bump down stairs, leap from one rooftop to another and drive through a sewer pipe, it proved the perfect getaway car in a busy city.

JAGUAR E-TYPE

Based on the D-Type which had won Le Mans three times in the 1950s, the E-Type sports car of 1961 was described by Enzo Ferrari as the most beautiful car ever made. It outgunned and outshone everything else in the market and became the upmarket icon of the swinging sixties, a role it got to reprise in the Austin Powers films between 1997 and 2002.

ASTON MARTIN DB5

Launched in 1963, the 4-litre DB5 is known the world over as the best Bond car ever, driven by the actor widely considered to be the best 007 ever (Sean Connery) in *Goldfinger* (1964) and *Thunderball* (1965). Reclining seats, twin fuel tanks and chrome wire wheels came as standard; machine guns and an ejector seat were extra. A DB5 used in the Bond films was sold in 2010 for £2.6 million.

LONDON TAXI

The licensed taxis of London are commonly referred to as black cabs in spite of the fact that many of them now appear in non-black colours. They have been roaming London for over a hundred years and are famous for their tight turning circle and the need for their drivers to pass The Knowledge test before being allowed to drive them.

LONDON TAXI IN NUMBERS

22,000
approximate number of London taxis

10 seconds
average time you can go without seeing one

£2.60
minimum fare for a London taxi ride in 2016

50
number of gold-coloured cabs produced to celebrate the Queen's Golden Jubilee in 2002

£20,000
amount of cash once left behind in the back of a cab (in £50 notes)

£39,995
starting price of the latest model (TX4 Euro 6) in 2016

25 feet
turning radius (originally necessary to negotiate the tight roundabout at the entrance to the Savoy Hotel)

12
number of colours a 'black cab' is available in today

Great British aircraft

From the iconic biplane flown in World War One (and by Biggles, every boy's favourite pilot adventurer) to the world's first supersonic airliner, British designers have been every bit as adept in the air as on land or sea.

SUPERMARINE SPITFIRE

The gutsy little Spitfire with the Rolls-Royce engine was the only British fighter plane in continuous production throughout World War Two. It was the backbone of RAF Fighter Command and was instrumental in beating back the Luftwaffe in the Battle of Britain. Its distinct thin, elliptical wings maximised its speed and manoeuvrability in the air.

PERFORMANCE CAPABILITY OF A SPITFIRE (MKII)

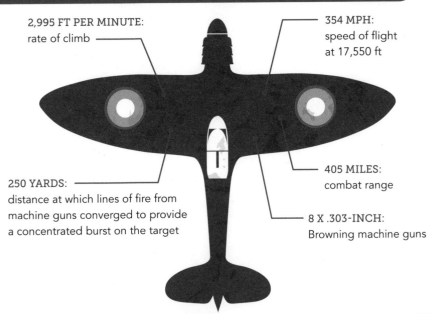

2,995 FT PER MINUTE: rate of climb

354 MPH: speed of flight at 17,550 ft

250 YARDS: distance at which lines of fire from machine guns converged to provide a concentrated burst on the target

405 MILES: combat range

8 X .303-INCH: Browning machine guns

HAWKER SIDDELEY HARRIER

The first attack aircraft capable of short and even vertical take-off and landing, commonly known as the Harrier Jump Jet. They were stationed in West Germany in the 1970s during the Cold War and used to good effect during the Falklands War in 1982.

SOPWITH CAMEL

The Sopwith Camel was a single-seater biplane fighter used on the Western Front in World War One, shooting down 1,249 enemy aircraft. It gained immortality as the plane flown in the W. E. Johns novels by Biggles of 266 Squadron.

CONCORDE

A joint effort between Britain and France, Concorde became the world's first supersonic airliner in 1976, flew for 27 years and achieved a record time of 2 hours 52 minutes 59 seconds between London and New York in 1996. Its adjustable nose allowed maximum streamlining when straight and afforded the flight crew visibility for take-off and landing when tilted.

CHAPTER 7

FOOD AND DRINK IN BRITAIN

They used to say a country is defined by what it eats and drinks, but it's getting a bit more complicated than that these days. Horizons have been broadened by travel, living in a multicultural society has added interest and variety to our diet, and there is a growing trend to fight back against the fat and sugar levels of the past. Let us start, however, with the unhealthiest diet of them all, the one that puts even the full English breakfast and the Ulster fry in the shade.

Traditional
Teapot

The Henry VIII diet

It probably wasn't a coincidence that Henry VIII ended up with a 54-inch waist, gout, diabetes and high blood pressure. Here is a feasible list of the more unusual dishes that were laid before him at a single sitting, to be washed down with copious amounts of ale and sweetened wine:

STARTER

- Boiled whale meat
- Baked lampreys
- Fillet of porpoise

MAIN COURSE

- Small whole-roasted birds (robin, sparrow, thrush, woodcock, quail, blackbird)
- Large whole-roasted birds (gull, crane, bittern, buzzard, pheasant, swan, peacock)
- Stew of badger
- Grilled beaver tails
- Organs (lungs, spleen, udders)

PUDDING

- Quinces stewed in honey
- Fat brambles in yellow cream
- Yeoman's bread pudding

War rations

From one extreme to the other, let's have a look at some smaller portions that might have had Henry VIII running about again in no time. These are the items your ration coupons would have allowed you to buy per person per week in April 1945:

MINISTRY 🅜🅕 OF FOOD
RATION BOOK

4 oz (113 g) bacon
4 oz (113 g) ham
One shilling and twopence worth of meat (approx. 540 g)
8 oz (226 g) sugar
2 oz (57 g) loose tea
2 oz (57 g) cheese (vegetarians were allowed an extra 3 oz on surrender of their meat, bacon and ham coupons)
8 oz (226 g) marmalade
2 oz (57 g) butter
4 oz (113 g) margarine
2 oz (57 g) lard
3 oz (85 g) sweets
1 egg (2 for expectant mothers, 3 for children and invalids)
3 pints of milk (given first to expectant mothers and children under five if supplies were low)

Note: contrary to what you might expect during times of rationing, the overall health of the British people improved, infant mortality rates declined and life expectancy rose (if you ignore deaths caused by the hostilities of the time).

National dishes

From the humble sandwich to the Sunday roast, Britain has given the world a lot more of its eating habits than many people realise. Here are just some of the foods we have blessed ourselves and other nations with:

FULL BREAKFAST

The Henry VIII way to start the day, with eggs, bacon and sausage, along with a host of regional added extras, all washed down with mugs of tea or coffee. So popular now that everywhere from greasy spoons to posh hotels around the world often serve an all-day version.

FISH AND CHIPS

The first fish and chip shop in Britain was opened in the East End of London in 1860 by Jewish immigrants who had the idea of serving chips with their traditional dish of fried fish. They soon became a nationwide staple thanks to the development of trawl fishing in the North Sea and the advent of the railways to transport the fish quickly around the country.

SANDWICH

Pretty much anything stuffed between two layers of bread, it got the name because the eighteenth-century aristocrat John Montagu, 4th Earl of Sandwich, needed his food served in a way that allowed him to continue playing cards without having to stop to eat something with a fork.

STEAK AND KIDNEY PUDDING OR PIE

Steak and kidney pudding (encased within suet pastry) dates back to the nineteenth century, but the later steak and kidney pie (beef, kidney and onion in a salted gravy flavoured with Worcestershire sauce and topped with pastry) is now more popular around the world.

SUNDAY ROAST

Originating as the traditional meal to be eaten after church on Sunday, the roast meat, potatoes and vegetables could all cook slowly during the service, just waiting to be served with gravy on the return home. Now also enjoyed the world over as pub grub, even by people who don't go to church.

THE GREAT BRITISH CURRY

Curry took off in Britain in the 1970s when it was served with chips after the pubs closed. It has since morphed into a British 'national dish', with flavours and strengths to suit every taste, and is available everywhere from takeaways and supermarkets to Michelin-starred Indian restaurants.

AFTERNOON TEA

Long before the advent of the coffee-shop culture in Britain, tearooms existed all over the country to serve the traditional afternoon tea with cucumber or egg-and-cress sandwiches, scones with clotted cream and jam, cakes, muffins, crumpets or shortbread. Afternoon tea has since become a luxury dining experience in top hotels around the world.

SPOTTED DICK

An early recipe dates to 1849 but no one seems to know who or what Dick was. The suet pudding containing currants and/ or raisins is traditionally served with custard.

Protected Geographical Indication (PGI)

More and more British manufacturers and growers are applying for PGI status to protect their age-old reputation and to eliminate any variants that claim to be what they're not. Here are some of those that have succeeded.

MELTON MOWBRAY PORK PIE

The Melton Mowbray version of this cold meat pie must contain uncured pork and be encased in a hand-formed hot-water crust pastry, otherwise it's just a pork pie.

ARBROATH SMOKIES

Local legend says a haddock store caught fire one night in Arbroath and that the fish trapped and smoked inside their barrels were found to be rather tasty the next morning.

WHITSTABLE OYSTERS

Must be farmed in the Thames Estuary between Shoeburyness and North Foreland. Once the food of the poor in the nineteenth century, they are now an expensive delicacy.

STILTON CHEESE

Only Stilton made to a strict code in Derbyshire, Leicestershire and Nottinghamshire can be called Stilton. Cheese made in Stilton, therefore, is not allowed to be called Stilton.

CORNISH PASTY

Seasoned beef, potatoes, swede and onion baked in a crimped semi-circle of shortcrust pastry was popular with Cornish tin miners because it made for a whole meal that could be carried and eaten easily.

COMBER EARLIES

When the new potatoes of this Northern Irish crop arrive each year, a festival is held in the town of Comber to mark the occasion. Highlights include 'interactive potato sampling'.

STORNOWAY BLACK PUDDING

To be the real thing, it has to be made in the Stornoway area of the Scottish island of Lewis and Harris. Its meaty texture and flavour derives from the oatmeal used to hold the beef suet, onion and blood together.

ECCLES CAKE

A flaky butter pastry with currants first sold in the town of Eccles, Greater Manchester, in 1793. So tasty they named Spike Milligan's *Goon Show* character and my in-laws after it.

ANGLESEY SEA SALT

Halen Mon, or Anglesey Sea Salt, is the additive-free salt harvested from the pure seawater of the Menai Strait in North Wales.

Celebrity cooking

Ever since *Mrs Beeton's Book of Household Management* sold two million copies in 1868, recipe books have been big business in Britain and more and more cooks, chefs and bakers have enjoyed celebrity status.

FANNY CRADOCK

Selling cookery books in record numbers and never off the television in the post-war decades, Fanny Cradock cooked with her apron over fantastic ballgowns while insulting her bumbling husband Johnnie. Credited with concocting the prawn cocktail.

JANE ASHER

Having gained early fame as a child actress in the 1950s, Jane Asher carved out a career in film and TV, but also found time to write best-selling novels and cake-decorating books, and to set up a company that provided party cakes for special occasions.

DELIA SMITH

Having baked the cake that appeared on the 1969 Rolling Stones album cover for *Let It Bleed*, Delia Smith went on to become Britain's best-selling cookery author and a majority shareholder of her beloved Norwich City Football Club.

MARCO PIERRE WHITE

Dubbed the first celebrity chef, this working-class boy from Leeds became a top restaurateur and the youngest chef ever – at the age of 33 in 1995 – to receive three Michelin stars.

NIGEL SLATER

The celebrity status of this food writer, journalist and broadcaster became such that the BBC made the 2010 film *Toast* based on the autobiographical novel about his childhood.

TWO FAT LADIES

TV cooks Clarissa Dickson Wright and Jennifer Paterson roamed the country in the 1990s on a Triumph Thunderbird motorbike driven by Paterson while Dickson Wright sat alongside in a double-wide sidecar. Lean cuisine was not their thing as they cooked food for entire schools or army garrisons.

THE HAIRY BIKERS

The male answer to the Two Fat Ladies, David Myers and Simon King have forged a TV career by combining motorbike travelling with cooking and cheerful bantering around the world since 2004.

GORDON RAMSAY

With 16 Michelin stars on his restaurants, the celebrity chef is equally well known for his TV rants and raves whenever his pupils don't get something quite right. If you can't stand the heat, according to Ramsay, you should get out of the kitchen!

NIGELLA LAWSON

The daughter of former Chancellor of the Exchequer Nigel Lawson, the self-styled Domestic Goddess has sold more than three million cookery books and fronted 11 TV series in the past 20 years.

JAMIE OLIVER

The champion of English cuisine landed his first TV programme *The Naked Chef* in 1999 and hasn't looked back since. His Feed Me Better campaign has embarrassed the British government into providing healthier school meals for children.

MARY BERRY AND PAUL HOLLYWOOD

Food writer Mary Berry and head baker Paul Hollywood were the judges of the BAFTA-winning amateur baking competition *The Great British Bake Off* between 2010 and 2016. Credited with renewing interest in baking throughout Britain.

What the British drink

Although the Romans introduced wine and the Anglo-Saxons brought ale, it was ultimately tea that was to become the British national drink for three centuries, although that is by no means all that Britons have been drinking to quench their thirst, cheer themselves up or drown their sorrows.

TEA

When the British took to drinking tea in the seventeenth century, they simply couldn't get enough of it, so they started to produce it in huge quantities themselves in India. It remains one of the most popular drinks across Britain today.

COFFEE

Since the 1990s Britons have embraced the coffee culture many of us first encountered through the US sitcom *Friends*, and now 70 million cups are drunk in the country each day.

BEER

Through Anglo-Saxon mead halls and medieval coaching inns to the pubs of today, Britons have enjoyed their beer for centuries. The craft beer revolution of recent years has introduced every type of beer imaginable to the British palate.

SCOTCH WHISKY

Distilled for centuries from cereals, water and yeast, but getting its colour from caramel, the name whisky derives from the Gaelic for 'water of life'. Protected Geographical Indication status ensures that Scotch whisky is only produced in Scotland.

GIN

Dutch gin replaced French brandy when William of Orange arrived to take the British throne in 1688. Londoners soon began to make their own brands, which have gone on to be popular the world over.

WINE

Although there are now hundreds of vineyards around Britain, we still import more than any other country in order to satisfy our seemingly insatiable demand, so the Romans have a lot to answer for after bringing it here in the first place.

Royal Warrants of Appointment

Every producer dreams of receiving an Appointment to HM the Queen or other senior member of the Royal Family, for therein lies fame and fortune. If it's good enough for the Royal Family, it's certainly good enough for us plebs! Here are some of those lucky enough to enjoy the privilege:

- **Cadbury UK:** keeping the Queen in Creme Eggs since 1969

- **Fortnum & Mason:** providing high-class groceries to the Queen and the Prince of Wales since 1955

- **HP Foods:** supplier of brown sauce for the Queen's chips since 1951

- **Laphroaig Distillery, Islay:** topping up the Prince of Wales with single malt whisky since 1994

- **Schweppes Holdings:** making sure successive monarchs didn't have to drink their gin neat since the nineteenth century

- **Shepherd Neame, Kent:** drunk since 1998 by the Prince of Wales, presumably with a Laphroaig chaser

- **Twinings & Co:** providing successive monarchs with a nice cup of tea since Queen Victoria's accession in 1837

- **Waitrose:** first supermarket to be granted a Royal Warrant by the Queen after the Windsor branch started sending stuff up to the castle in 2002

- **Harrods of Knightsbridge:** had Royal Warrants from 1910 to 2000, which were withdrawn after then owner Mohamed Al-Fayed burned them to rid himself of the 'curse' they had brought upon his family (his son died alongside Princess Diana in a car crash in Paris in 1997)

CHAPTER 8

BRITISH SPORTING HIGHLIGHTS

For such a small nation, British individuals and teams have left an indelible mark on a great many sports, from the first sub-4-minute mile to the most successful Olympic cyclists of all time. Let's have a look at some of our great British sporting heroes...

Cricket

Olympics

Our rowers used to reign supreme as the greatest British Olympians, but that was before a new breed of cyclists came along and blew them out of the water. Here are our most successful Olympians of all time (up to and including the Rio 2016 Games):

CHRIS HOY Track cycling 2000–12 Gold medals: 6 	**JASON KENNY** Track cycling 2008–16 Gold medals: 6 	**BRADLEY WIGGINS** Track and road cycling 2000–16 Gold medals: 5
STEVE REDGRAVE Rowing 1984–2000 Gold medals: 5 	**BEN AINSLIE** Sailing 1996–2012 Gold medals: 4 	**MO FARAH** Athletics 2012–16 Gold medals: 4
MATTHEW PINSENT Rowing 1992–2004 Gold medals: 4 	**PAULO RADMILOVIC** Water polo and swimming 1908–1920 Gold medals: 4 	**LAURA KENNY** Track cycling 2012–16 Gold medals: 4

OLYMPIC HIGHLIGHTS
(UP TO AND INCLUDING RIO 2016)

- London was the first city to host the modern Olympics three times, in 1908, 1948 and 2012.

- Britain finished in a quite astonishing second place at the 2016 Rio Olympics with 27 gold, 23 silver and 17 bronze medals, behind the USA and narrowly pipping China by just one gold medal.

- Britain's three top medal winners of all time are cyclists – Chris Hoy (6 gold), Jason Kenny (6 gold) and Bradley Wiggins (5 gold).

- Cyclist Laura Kenny is the most successful British female Olympian of all time, with four gold medals (see 'Cycling highlights'), followed closely by Charlotte Dujardin, who has three gold and one silver in equestrian dressage.

- Rowing legend Steve Redgrave is the only Olympian ever to win gold at five successive Olympics in an endurance event.

- Britain's greatest all-round athlete is Daley Thompson, with decathlon gold in 1980 and 1984.

- Princess Anne is the only member of the Royal Family to have competed at an Olympics, as part of the equestrian eventing team at the 1976 Montreal Games.

- Britain's most famous Winter Olympians are Jayne Torvill and Christopher Dean, who won ice-dancing gold at Sarajevo in 1984 with a row of perfect sixes for artistic impression after dancing to Ravel's 'Bolero'.

Paralympics

The Paralympic Games grew from the wheelchair sports events held at Stoke Mandeville hospital in Buckinghamshire for soldiers with spinal injuries. As at the end of the 2016 Rio Games, here are our most successful Paralympians to date:

MIKE KENNY
Swimming
1976–88
Gold medals: 16

SARAH STOREY
Swimming and cycling
1992–2016
Gold medals: 14

DAVID ROBERTS
Swimming
2000–08
Gold medals: 11

TANNI GREY-THOMPSON
Wheelchair racing
1992–2004
Gold medals: 11

LEE PEARSON
Equestrian
2000–16
Gold medals: 11

CAROL BRYANT
Wheelchair racing, table tennis, fencing and swimming
1992–2004
Gold medals: 10

ISABEL NEWSTEAD
Swimming, shooting and athletics
1980–2004
Gold medals: 10

PARALYMPIC HIGHLIGHTS

- Swimmer Mike Kenny, Britain's most successful Paralympian to date, won his 16 gold medals at four consecutive Games.

- Britain's most famous Paralympian, Tanni Grey-Thompson, went on to take her place in the House of Lords and be a great worldwide ambassador for disability sports.

- Swimmer Ellie Simmonds won the first two of her five gold medals to date when she competed at the 2008 Beijing Games at the age of just 13.

- Britain's first Winter Paralympic gold was won at the Sochi 2014 Games by visually impaired skier Kelly Gallagher.

Football

The world's most popular spectator sport was first documented in England in 1409 and codified in London in 1863. We've all kicked a few balls since then, some more skilfully than others.

FOOTBALL HIGHLIGHTS

The oldest football club in the world is Sheffield FC, founded in 1857. They are currently playing in the Evo-Stik League First Division South.

The biggest crowd for a women's game was 53,000 in 1920, when Dick Kerr's Ladies of Preston beat St Helen's Ladies 4–0.

Stanley Matthews is considered the greatest footballer to have played the game, nicknamed the 'Wizard of the Dribble' during his long career with Stoke City and Blackpool. His performance in the 1953 FA Cup Final was so good it is still remembered as the 'Matthews Final'.

In 1963, Tottenham Hotspur became the first British team to win a European trophy, beating Atletico Madrid 5–1 in the final of the European Cup Winners' Cup.

In 1966 England won the World Cup at Wembley, beating West Germany 4–2 after extra time. West Ham's Geoff Hurst got the hat-trick that mattered.

In 1967 Glasgow Celtic became the first British club to win the European Cup (the forerunner to today's Champions League) after defeating Inter Milan 2–1 in Lisbon.

In 1976 Brian Clough took charge of English Second Division side Nottingham Forest and achieved the impossible by securing promotion in 1977, winning the First Division in 1978 and winning the European Cup in 1979 and 1980.

Manchester United have won the English league title 20 times, two more than Liverpool.

Liverpool have won the European Cup/Champions League five times, two more than Manchester United.

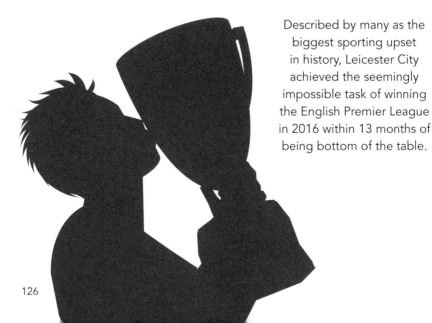

Described by many as the biggest sporting upset in history, Leicester City achieved the seemingly impossible task of winning the English Premier League in 2016 within 13 months of being bottom of the table.

Rugby

Ever since young William Webb Ellis supposedly picked up the ball and ran with it during a football match at Rugby School in 1823, the game of rugby has been putting football to shame with its lack of player histrionics coupled with total respect for the authority of the referee.

RUGBY UNION HIGHLIGHTS

The Home Nations Championship involving England, Ireland, Scotland and Wales was first played in 1883. It has since morphed into the Six Nations Championship to incorporate France and Italy.

The Calcutta Cup, awarded to the winner of the annual match between Scotland and England, is made from melted-down Indian rupees and decorated with cobras and an elephant.

England defeated the host nation Australia to win the Rugby World Cup in 2003, thanks to a last-minute drop goal by Jonny Wilkinson at the end of extra time.

England dominates women's rugby and won the World Cup in 2014. Around 20,000 women now play the game at various levels across the country.

Rugby union is the national sport of Wales and their supporters are renowned for the quality of their singing.

RUGBY LEAGUE HIGHLIGHTS

Rugby league broke away from rugby union in 1895 to allow its working-class players in northern England to get paid for playing as they could ill afford to take time off for training or recovering from injury.

Great Britain won the Rugby League World Cup three times, in 1954, 1960 and 1972, but in 2007 the British national team was replaced by separate teams to represent England, Scotland and Wales.

Wigan Warriors are the most successful club team to date, having won the League Championship for the 21st time in 2016, and the Challenge Cup for the 20th time in 2013.

Winger Jason Robinson was the greatest convert from rugby league to rugby union when he switched codes in 2000, winning 19 international caps as a league player before adding 51 as a union player.

Cricket

Having originated in the south-east of England in the Middle Ages, it became England's national sport in the eighteenth century. The formal laws it still adheres to today were established at the Marylebone Cricket Club (MCC) at Lord's in 1835, and passion for the game has since spread around the globe. Here are just some of the highlights of English cricket in that time.

CRICKET HIGHLIGHTS

- The career of amateur cricketer W. G. Grace spanned a remarkable 44 years (1865–1908) and he is widely considered to be the first great all-rounder. His skill and technique has had a lasting legacy on how the game should be played.

- C. B. Fry is best remembered for a first-class cricket career spanning 27 years (1894–1921) and 95 Test matches, but he also played football for England, equalled the world long-jump record and played rugby for Oxford University.

- England hold the biggest ever win margin in a Test match, having beaten Australia at the Oval in 1938 by an innings and 579 runs.

- Jim Laker holds the record for best bowling figures in a single innings, with 10–53 against Australia at Old Trafford in 1956, and for best bowling figures in a Test match, with 19–90 in that same match.

- Ian Botham is England's best ever all-rounder, with a Test record of 5,200 runs, 14 centuries, 383 wickets and 120 catches. In one Test match against India in Mumbai in 1980, he scored a century and bowled 13 100.

- Graham Gooch holds the world record for most runs scored in a Test match, 456 against India at Lord's in 1990.

- After England lost at home to Australia for the first time in 1882, a mock newspaper obituary declared that English cricket had died and that 'the body will be cremated and the ashes taken to Australia'. The sides have been playing for 'the Ashes' ever since.

- As at the end of the 2015 Ashes series, which England won, England has won 32 series, Australia has won 32 series and five have been drawn.

- The England women's team have won the Women's Cricket World Cup three times already, in 1973, 1993 and 2009.

Tennis

Court tennis and real tennis were favourite pastimes of the young Henry VIII at Hampton Court and were the precursors of the lawn tennis game established in 1875. British tennis history is inextricably bound up in the Wimbledon championships.

TENNIS HIGHLIGHTS

- The first Wimbledon championships were in 1877 (men's) and 1884 (women's).

- The Queen isn't a huge tennis fan, but her dad (George VI) played in the doubles at Wimbledon in 1926 when he was still the Duke of York.

- British player Fred Perry won 14 Grand Slam titles, including three consecutive Wimbledon singles titles (1934–36).

- In 1977, the year of Wimbledon's centenary and the Queen's Silver Jubilee, Virginia Wade won the ladies' singles, her fourth and final Grand Slam singles title.

- Three players have won the men's singles a record seven times: William Renshaw (GB) 1881–89; Pete Sampras (USA) 1993–2000; and Roger Federer (Switzerland) 2003–12.

- Martina Navratilova (Czech Republic/USA) won the ladies' singles a record nine times (1978–90).

- An exception was made to their all-white tennis attire rule when Wimbledon hosted the London 2012 Olympics tournament, as players appeared in their national team's colours.

- The longest professional tennis match on record was at Wimbledon in 2010, when the American John Isner finally defeated Frenchman Nicolas Mahut 6–4, 3–6, 6–7, 7–6, 70–68 after 11 hours and 5 minutes over three days.

- British player Andy Murray became world number one in 2016, having already won three Grand Slams (including two Wimbledon titles) and two Olympic gold medals.

2016 WIMBLEDON IN NUMBERS

493,928
total attendance

68 (20)
temperature (in °F and °C respectively) balls stored at

177,135
glasses of Pimm's

54,250
tennis balls

133,800
scones

250 ball boys and girls

7,000
litres of cream

139,435
portions of strawberries

2,772
weight in kilos of bananas (for the players)

1,800
catering staff

858 Hawk-Eye challenges by players (with 26.7 per cent success rate)

Golf

In 1471 James II of Scotland issued a decree banning golf because it interfered with archery practice when there was probably a war with England coming up, but Scotland was the home of golf and the sport had already gripped the nation. It was only a matter of time before it spread to England and then the rest of the world.

GOLFING HIGHLIGHTS

When James VI of Scotland moved to London in 1603 to also become James I of England, his court brought their golf clubs with them and in no time at all golf caught on south of the border.

The Royal and Ancient Golf Club of St Andrews was founded in 1754 and codified the rules of golf in 1897.

Englishman Nick Faldo is Britain's most successful golfer, having won six majors and having played more Ryder Cup matches (11) and won more Ryder Cup points (25) than any other golfer on either side.

English golfer Laura Davies is Britain's most successful female player, having won four majors between 1987 and 1996, and having been the first non-American to top the LPGA money list.

In 2016, when golf returned to the Olympics after an absence of 112 years in Rio de Janeiro, English player Justin Rose won the gold medal and shot a hole-in-one while he was about it.

THE OPEN CHAMPIONSHIP IN NUMBERS

1860
the year in which Willie Park won the first championship, at Prestwick

46
age at which 'Old' Tom Morris became the oldest winner in 1867

6
record number of Open wins, achieved by Jersey's Harry Vardon between 1896 and 1914

17
age at which 'Young' Tom Morris (son of 'Old' Tom Morris) became the youngest ever winner in 1868

59
age at which American Tom Watson had an 8-ft putt on the final green in 2009 to equal Harry Vardon's record of six Open Championships, but he sadly missed the putt and ended up second

2
number of Open Championships won by players from Northern Ireland within four years, Darren Clarke in 2011 and Rory McIlroy in 2014

−19
lowest ever score under par, scored by American Tiger Woods when he won at St Andrews in 2000

Cycling

The popularity of cycling at every level in Britain has exploded as a result of staggeringly good results at the Olympic Games and the Tour de France. Here are some cool facts about the people who have made the difference.

Having secured unprecedented success for Team GB at Olympic level, cycling coach Dave Brailsford set up Team Sky in 2009 and delivered the first British winner of the Tour de France (Bradley Wiggins) in 2012.

Track cyclists Chris Hoy and Jason Kenny are the most successful British Olympians of all time, having both won six gold medals and one silver.

As of 2016, Bradley Wiggins is Britain's most decorated Olympian, having won five gold, one silver and two bronze. He is also the only cyclist to win an Olympic gold medal and the Tour de France in the same year (2012).

Chris Froome of Team Sky has won the Tour de France three times at the time of writing, completely destroying the opposition in 2013, 2015 and 2016.

Mark Cavendish is the most successful British sprinter in Tour de France history. He had already amassed 30 stage wins by the end of the 2016 Tour, only four less than the legendary Belgian Eddy Merckx.

After winning two track cycling gold medals at the London 2012 Games and the same again at Rio in 2016, Laura Kenny became Britain's most successful female Olympian of all time.

Running

From the 100-m sprint to the marathon distance of 26 miles 264 yards, Britain has seen a lot of its runners speed to success in the fast lane.

RUNNING IN NUMBERS

1 mile
Roger Bannister famously broke the four-minute barrier on 6 May 1954, when he ran the mile at Oxford University's Iffley Road Track in 3 minutes 59.4 seconds.

5,000 and 10,000 metres
distance runner Mo Farah is the most successful British track athlete in history, having secured the 'quadruple double' by winning gold in both the 5,000 and 10,000 m at successive Olympic and World Championships.

100 metres
sprinter Linford Christie is the only British runner to win the 100 m at all four major levels – Olympic, World, European and Commonwealth.

2 hours 15 minutes 25 seconds
women's marathon world record set by Paula Radcliffe in the 2003 London Marathon. The record still stands at the time of writing in 2017.

800 metres and 1,500 metres
middle-distance runner Kelly Holmes overcame injury and clinical depression to win double gold in these events at the 2004 Athens Olympics.

1,500 metres
middle-distance runner Sebastian Coe won gold in the 1,500 m at the Moscow 1980 Olympics and again at the 1984 Olympics in Los Angeles.

110 metres
Colin Jackson won gold in the 110 m hurdles at two World Championships and set a world record in 1993 that stood for ten years.

CHAPTER 9

BRITAIN IN THE ARTS

From Shakespeare to J. K. Rowling, from Elgar to the Beatles, from J. M. W. Turner to David Hockney, British creative geniuses have been enlightening the world for centuries.

Bayeux
Tapestry

Literature

Before the days of the printing press, classic works were beautifully handwritten and illustrated, notably *The Ecclesiastical History of the English People* by the Venerable Bede in the eighth century and *The Anglo-Saxon Chronicle* of the ninth century. Within two years of William Caxton introducing the printing press to Britain in 1476, mass-produced British literature was up and running with *The Canterbury Tales* of Geoffrey Chaucer. It would take William Shakespeare to really set the world alight, though.

WILLIAM SHAKESPEARE (1564–1616)

Hundreds
new phrases introduced that are still in common use today

11 histories brought to life

36 number of plays in the First Folio, published in 1623

12.5 his percentage share in the Globe Theatre (completed 1599)

1,700 new words introduced to the English language

154 number of sonnets penned

12 tragedies evoked to remind people that their lives could be far worse

38 number of plays written

14 comedies produced to lift the gloom of harsh Elizabethan life

1,224 characters created

SEVENTEENTH CENTURY

The seventeenth century majored in the King James Bible, the metaphysical poetry of Johns Donne and Milton, and the diaries of Samuel Pepys.

WRITER	BEST-KNOWN WORK
Ben Jonson	*Volpone* or *The Fox* (1606)
Samuel Pepys	*The Diary of Samuel Pepys* (1660–69)
John Milton	*Paradise Lost* (1667)
John Bunyan	*The Pilgrim's Progress* (1678)
John Donne	Works of poetry and satire

EIGHTEENTH CENTURY

From this century, we got the satire of Jonathan Swift, the earliest modern novels of Henry Fielding and Daniel Defoe, and the legacy of poet and songwriter Robert Burns.

WRITER	BEST-KNOWN WORK
Alexander Pope	*The Rape of the Lock* (1714)
Daniel Defoe	*Robinson Crusoe* (1719)
Henry Fielding	*The History of Tom Jones, a Foundling* (1749)
Samuel Johnson	*A Dictionary of the English Language* (1755)
Samuel Taylor Coleridge	*The Rime of the Ancient Mariner* (1798)
Robert Burns	Folk songs and poetry

NINETEENTH CENTURY

The Romantic poetry of Wordsworth, Byron, Keats and Shelley enjoyed its time in the limelight, fiction really took off with the genius of Charles Dickens and the novels of Jane Austen and the Brontë sisters, and the detective novel was born with Wilkie Collins' *The Moonstone*.

WRITER	BEST-KNOWN WORK
William Wordsworth	*I Wandered Lonely as a Cloud* (1804)
William Blake	*Jerusalem* (1804)
Lord Byron	*Childe Harold's Pilgrimage* (1812–18)
Jane Austen	*Pride and Prejudice* (1813)
Walter Scott	*Rob Roy* (1817)
Mary Shelley	*Frankenstein* (1818)
Charlotte Brontë	*Jane Eyre* (1847)
Emily Brontë	*Wuthering Heights* (1847)
William Makepeace Thackeray	*Vanity Fair* (1848)
Charles Dickens	*Great Expectations* (1861)
Lewis Carroll	*Alice's Adventures in Wonderland* (1865)
Wilkie Collins	*The Moonstone* (1868)
George Eliot	*Middlemarch* (1872)
Robert Louis Stevenson	*Treasure Island* (1883)
Thomas Hardy	*Tess of the D'Urbervilles* (1892)
Arthur Conan Doyle	*The Adventures of Sherlock Holmes* (1892)
Rudyard Kipling	*The Jungle Book* (1894)
Oscar Wilde	*The Importance of Being Earnest* (1895)
H. G. Wells	*The War of the Worlds* (1898)

TWENTIETH CENTURY

The literary world went a bit anti-establishment with the likes of D. H. Lawrence, George Orwell, T. S. Eliot and Dylan Thomas cocking a snoop at the powers that be, but less political writers like Agatha Christie and P. G. Wodehouse kept the mood a bit lighter. Here are just some of the bumper crop of writers that provided the twentieth-century British literary canon:

WRITER	BEST-KNOWN WORK
E. M. Forster	*A Room with a View* (1908)
Wilfred Owen	*Dulce et Decorum Est* (1917)
P. G. Wodehouse	*Jeeves and Wooster series* (1919–71)
T. S. Eliot	*The Waste Land* (1922)
Virginia Woolf	*Mrs Dalloway* (1925)
D. H. Lawrence	*Lady Chatterley's Lover* (1928)
Agatha Christie	*Murder on the Orient Express* (1934)
Graham Greene	*Brighton Rock* (1938)
George Orwell	*1984* (1949)
Doris Lessing	*The Grass is Singing* (1950)
Daphne du Maurier	*The Birds* (1952)
Dylan Thomas	*Under Milk Wood* (1954)
William Golding	*Lord of the Flies* (1954)
J. R. R. Tolkien	*The Lord of the Rings* (1955)
Philip Larkin	*The Whitsun Weddings* (1964)
John le Carré	*Tinker Tailor Soldier Spy* (1974)
Salman Rushdie	*Midnight's Children* (1981)
Terry Pratchett	Discworld series (1983–2015)

BRITISH LITERATURE TRIVIA

- Eighteenth-century novelist Daniel Defoe worked as a spy around Europe (but mostly in Edinburgh) for Queen Mary II and William III.

- Robert Burns' 1788 poem 'Auld Lang Syne' is still sung around the world every year at the stroke of midnight on Hogmanay (New Year's Eve), and his 'Address to a Haggis' is likewise recited annually the world over on 25 January (Burns Night).

- The Brontë sisters originally wrote under pseudonyms due to a prejudice against female writers in nineteenth-century Britain. They did at least manage to maintain their own initials, though.

AUTHOR	PSEUDONYM	MOST FAMOUS NOVEL
Charlotte Brontë	Currer Bell	*Jane Eyre*
Emily Brontë	Ellis Bell	*Wuthering Heights*
Anne Brontë	Acton Bell	*The Tenant of Wildfell Hall*

- Charles Dickens wrote 4.6 million words and created 3,592 characters in his stories. *The Oxford English Dictionary* attributes 9,218 words or expressions to him, including 'artful dodger', 'butterfingers', 'devil-may-care' and 'slowcoach'.

- Jane Austen's novels have rarely been out of print since her death in 1817, and she is commemorated on the £10 note coming into circulation 200 years on, in 2017.

- Worried that female writers were stereotyped as producers of lighthearted romance, Mary Ann Evans wrote under the pseudonym of George Eliot in order to be taken seriously.

- J. K. Rowling has written the best-selling book series of all time, Harry Potter, with over 500 million sold worldwide and the books translated into 73 languages.

- Since records began to be kept, the three best-selling authors in the world are all British: William Shakespeare (*c.* 4 billion books sold); Agatha Christie (*c.* 4 billion books sold); and Barbara Cartland (*c.* 1 billion books sold).

Music

Although singing as a form of Christian worship and minstrels playing at court had been happening for a long time, structured music really took off in Britain when German-born George Frideric Handel turned up to take out British citizenship in the nineteenth century.

CLASSICAL MUSIC

From the placid compositions of Thomas Tallis to the reactionary style of Peter Maxwell Davies, British composers have been producing meaningful music on and off for 500 years.

1532: Thomas Tallis was appointed organist at Dover Priory. He goes on to compose choral music for four successive monarchs of England.

1677: Henry Purcell was appointed composer to Charles II's string orchestra. He also composed over a hundred songs for the royal court, the Church and the stage.

1895: The first Proms season was held in London, with Henry Wood conducting the orchestra he himself had put together.

1901: Edward Elgar produced the first of his *Pomp and Circumstance Marches*, including the 'Land of Hope and Glory' section which is still given a lively rendition each year on the Last Night of the Proms at the Royal Albert Hall.

1916: Hubert Parry put William Blake's poem 'Jerusalem' to music. It has since been taken up as an anthem by the suffragette movement, the Labour Party conference and the England cricket team.

1916: Gustav Holst completed his orchestral suite *The Planets*.

1980: Peter Maxwell Davies composed the cabaret-style *Yellow Cake Revue* to protest against plans to mine for uranium ore in the Orkneys.

2016: Ralph Vaughan Williams' 1914 composition *The Lark Ascending* is voted number one in the Classic FM Hall of Fame for the third year running by around 170,000 listeners.

POPULAR MUSIC

The twentieth-century worldwide music revolution brought a whole lot of new music to the attention of the British public and inspired an ongoing catalogue of great British performers. Let's have a look at some music trivia that reflects a tiny fraction of their output.

Biggest-selling British artists

According to recorded sales figures (as opposed to the figures that artists or their fans claim), the five biggest-selling British artists of all time are as follows:

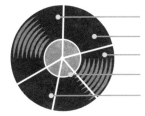

The Beatles: 270 million

Elton John: 167 million

Led Zeppelin: 139 million

Pink Floyd: 118 million

Queen: 109 million

British music in Guinness World Records

2 + 2: Adele is the first female artist to have two singles ('Someone Like You' and 'Rolling in the Deep') and two albums (*19* and *21*) in the UK top five simultaneously

3: British boy band One Direction are the first act in history to go straight to the top of the US Billboard album charts with their first three albums

62: the record number of hit singles in the UK charts, achieved by rock band Status Quo between 1968 and 2005

62 years 258 days: age of Tom Jones when he became the oldest winner of a Brit Award in 2003

100: most weeks spent at number one in the UK charts by a single record is Snow Patrol's 'Chasing Cars'

1,108,269: record number of singles sold in its first week in the UK charts is Will Young's 'Anything is Possible'

5,769,258: largest combined audience for a musical tour in 12 months, achieved by the Rolling Stones in 1994–95

17 years 304 days: age of Joss Stone when she became the youngest ever winner of a Brit Award in 2005

Art

Ever since Celtic monks illustrated the Lindisfarne Gospels around 700 CE, British artists have been creating masterpieces of one description or another. Here is but a tiny sample:

1070s: The Bayeux Tapestry illustrating the events leading up to and including the Battle of Hastings in 1066 was created in England, not Bayeux, in the 1070s, thereby rubbing salt into the wounds of the defeated nation.

1397: Richard II displayed illusions of heavenly grandeur by commissioning the Wilton Diptych depicting himself being presented to the Virgin Mary and the Baby Jesus.

1539: Henry VIII agreed to marry Anne of Cleves based on a portrait provided by his court painter Hans Holbein the Younger. Holbein was lucky to keep his head on his shoulders after Henry declared the real Anne to be rather less attractive than the portrait had suggested.

1768: Joshua Reynolds became the first president of the Royal Academy of Arts. His output as a painter was prolific, producing up to 150 portraits a year of the great and good of British society.

1821: Landscape painter John Constable produced *The Hay Wain*, his famous rural scene of the River Stour where it divides Suffolk and Essex.

1839: Landscape and maritime painter J. M. W. Turner put his command of light and colour to great effect in producing *The Fighting Temeraire*, which will be appearing behind him on the Bank of England's new £20 note, due to be in circulation by 2020.

1903: The Willow Tearooms designed in the Arts and Crafts style by architect, artist and designer Charles Rennie Mackintosh opened in Glasgow.

1929: Sculptor Henry Moore used Portland stone to complete his first public commission, *West Wind*, for the London Underground Headquarters building in London, but he is today best known for his monumental bronze sculptures.

1967: David Hockney, an influential contributor to the Pop Art movement of the 1960s, completed *A Bigger Splash*, representing the ubiquitous swimming pool of the Californian lifestyle he was then enjoying.

1991: Damien Hirst produced *The Physical Impossibility of Death in the Mind of Someone Living*, a controversial artwork consisting of a tiger shark preserved in formaldehyde inside a glass case.

Theatre, opera and ballet

After the Romans introduced theatre to Britain, biblical plays became popular in the Middle Ages until they were replaced by 'miracle plays' to cheer people up after the Black Death. Drama took off in Elizabethan times when William Shakespeare arrived on the scene (pun intended), and opera and ballet came to the fore at Covent Garden in the nineteenth century.

THEATRE

We already looked at Shakespeare in our Literature section, so let's have a closer look at some of the other great contributions to British drama since theatre once more rose to prominence in more recent times.

1741: Debut performance of actor, playwright and theatre manager David Garrick, who introduced a more natural style of acting and led the drive to make audiences behave in a more civilised fashion.

1852: First music hall (the Canterbury) opened in London, the beginning of a hundred years of variety entertainment that included popular song, speciality acts and comedy.

1861: Theatre producer Richard D'Oyly Carte built the Savoy Theatre, where he promoted Gilbert and Sullivan's comic operas, including *H. M. S. Pinafore*, *The Pirates of Penzance* and *The Mikado*.

1925: Anglo-Irish playwright George Bernard Shaw was awarded the Nobel Prize in Literature, having injected a degree of realism into British theatre. His best remembered play is *Pygmalion* (1913).

1930: West End debut of Laurence Olivier, arguably the most creative and versatile actor ever to tread the boards. He was equally at home with tragedy and comedy.

1931: Noel Coward wrote his famous song about 'Mad Dogs and Englishmen' going out in the midday sun while driving from Hanoi to Saigon. It was just one of the many songs, plays and theatre musical lyrics he set in the high society in which he lived his life.

1947: First Edinburgh Festival Fringe, responsible annually for providing offbeat entertainment and as a launchpad for successful careers, including Peter Cook, Dudley Moore, Derek Jacobi, Tom Stoppard and Billy Connolly.

1952: First performance of Agatha Christie's murder mystery *The Mousetrap* (then starring Richard Attenborough), now the longest-running play in the world after more than 26,000 performances in London's West End.

1957: Playwright, actor and director Harold Pinter comes to prominence with *The Room*, the first of his 'comedies of menace'.

1968: Composer and theatre impresario Andrew Lloyd Webber hit the big time with *Joseph and the Amazing Technicolour Dreamcoat*, which would be followed by many other hit musicals including *Jesus Christ Superstar* (1971), *Evita* (1978), *Cats* (1981) and *The Phantom of the Opera* (1986).

OPERA AND BALLET

After the two previous theatres on the site had been destroyed by fire, the current Royal Opera House at Covent Garden opened in 1858. At the end of World War Two the Royal Ballet company joined forces with the Royal Opera company within the theatre, beginning a marriage made in heaven that is still going strong today.

The French grand opera *Les Huguenots* by Giacomo Meyerbeer was the first production of the Royal Opera House.

Under the direction of Anglo-Irish dancer and choreographer Ninette de Valois (real name Edris Stannus), the Royal Ballet first performed as the Vic-Wells Ballet at London's Old Vic theatre in 1931, followed by another performance at Sadler's Wells theatre a few days later.

During World War One the Royal Opera House was used as a furniture depository and during World War Two it was converted into a Mecca Dance Hall to keep spirits up.

The theatre reopened in 1946 with a gala performance of Tchaikovsky's *Sleeping Beauty*, with Margot Fonteyn as Aurora.

Plácido Domingo, Luciano Pavarotti, Bryn Terfel and Joan Sutherland are just some of the big names to have sung with the Royal Opera.

Margot Fonteyn (real name Margaret Hookham) became the prima ballerina assoluta of the Royal Ballet, having joined the company in 1933 and famously teaming up with Rudolf Nureyev after he defected to the West in 1961.

Twenty years a principal dancer with the Royal Ballet, prima ballerina Darcey Bussell remains in the public eye as a judge on the BBC's *Strictly Come Dancing*.

British film, TV and radio

Britons like to entertain and be entertained, whatever the size of screen, or even with no screen at all in the case of radio. Let's have a look at just some of the programmes, films, actors and comedians that have made successive generations of us laugh, cry or be amazed.

FILM

Ever since we sent Charlie Chaplin over the pond to boost the silent movie era, we have been supplying Hollywood with a steady stream of actors, actresses and directors. Quite a few of them have even picked up Oscars.

Brits at the Oscars

 As of 2016, Brits have won 19 Best Actor, 16 Best Actress and 12 Best Director Academy Awards.

 Daniel Day-Lewis is the most successful British actor at the Oscars, with three Best Actor Academy Awards.

 Judi Dench holds the British record for number of Academy Award nominations (7), but has only won once, as Best Supporting Actress for *Shakespeare in Love* (1998).

 The 24 James Bond films up to *Spectre* (2016) had won five Oscars between them and are the third-highest-grossing film series of all time, behind Marvel Universe and Harry Potter.

BAFTA Film Awards

The BAFTA (British Academy of Film and Television Arts) Film Awards have been the British equivalent of the Oscars since 1948. As of 2016, the most successful recipients have been Peter Finch (five wins) and Maggie Smith (four wins).

British film industry

There are three major film studios within the corridor of the M25, the orbital motorway that encircles Greater London: Shepperton, Pinewood and Warner Brothers.

Shepperton Studios have been filming classics since 1931, including *Lawrence of Arabia*, *The Omen*, *Blade Runner*, *Gandhi*, *Out of Africa*, *Four Weddings and a Funeral*, *Love Actually*, *The Da Vinci Code*, *Gladiator*, *Gravity* and two *Star Wars* films.

Pinewood Studios are best known and loved for the bawdy *Carry On!* films made between 1958 and 1992 and most of the James Bond 007 films that began with *Dr No* in 1962, when the original 007 was Sean Connery.

Warner Bros. Studio produced blockbusters like the 007 film *Goldeneye*, the *Star Wars* prequels and Batman flick *The Dark Knight*, but really hit the big, big time with *Harry Potter and the Philosopher's Stone* in 2001, the first of eight Harry Potter films that would be made there over a ten-year period.

The film and TV industry in Northern Ireland has hit the big time in recent years as a location and production centre for films, and for TV productions like the blockbuster HBO fantasy series *Game of Thrones*, much of which is shot and produced there.

TV and radio

Be it comedy, drama, music, reality TV, the natural world, soap opera or game show, no stone has been left unturned in providing the British public with a bewildering choice of TV and radio programmes since Guglielmo Marconi first introduced radio to Britain in 1920 and John Logie Baird did likewise with commercial TV in 1928. In the 1990s the British TV offering increased from a handful of channels to the 500 or so now available.

MOST-WATCHED TV

Here are some of the most significant programmes to have gripped the British viewing public over the years.

Blue Peter: kicked off in 1958 and is now the longest-running children's TV show in the world, famous for making rudimentary arts and crafts out of everyday objects.

Coronation Street: Britain's soap-opera obsession took off in 1960 with the airing of the show that focuses on the residents of Weatherfield (based on Salford, Greater Manchester). It is now the longest-running TV soap opera in the world.

Doctor Who: ever since the first Time Lord (William Hartnell) took to the TARDIS in 1963, a dozen Doctors, armed with just their ingenuity and a sonic screwdriver, have been saving earth from the Daleks and other evil forces.

Top of the Pops: the weekly fix of top pop hits, usually mimed by their artists in the BBC studio, ran from 1964 to 2006 and still exists as an annual special on Christmas Day.

1966 World Cup Final: The most-watched one-off event in Britain was the 1966 World Cup final, when England beat West Germany 4–2 after extra time. It had 32.3 million viewers, which narrowly pips the 32.1 million who watched the funeral of Diana, Princess of Wales in 1997.

The Morecambe and Wise Show: between 1968 and 1983 the comic genius of Eric Morecambe and his straight-man partner Ernie Wise entertained the nation, attracting up to 28 million viewers with their Christmas specials.

Dad's Army: it ran for nine series between 1968 and 1977, following the trials and tribulations of a World War Two Home Guard platoon in the fictional seaside town of Walmington-on-Sea.

Monty Python's Flying Circus: the surreal comedy sketches of the Python team (1969–74) included the Dead Parrot and the Ministry of Silly Walks. Monty Python is so ingrained in our culture that questions relating to the programme have been included in the British Citizenship test.

Fawlty Towers: there were only two series (1975 and 1979), but no one can ever forget rude hotel owner Basil Fawlty (John Cleese), his long-suffering wife Sybil (Prunella Scales) and the hapless Spanish waiter Manuel (Andrew Sachs).

Yes Minister (1980–84) and Yes, Prime Minister (1986–87): this satirical political sitcom was Margaret Thatcher's favourite programme while she was in office.

Only Fools and Horses: a sitcom that began in 1981 following the antics of Robin Reliant-driving Del Boy and his brother Rodney as they tried to make ends meet with Trotters Independent Trading. It got the highest ever viewing figure for a British sitcom episode (24.3 million for the Christmas special in 1996).

EastEnders: Starting in 1985, it had the most-watched episode of a British TV series ever (30.2 million) on Christmas Day in 1986 when Dirty Den served divorce papers on his wife Angie in the Queen Vic.

The Office: the mockumentary sitcom about the working lives of the staff in the Slough branch of the Wernham Hogg Paper Company aired in 2001 and 2002. It became one of the biggest ever British TV exports around the world and was remade for American television, where it ran for nine series.

Planet Earth: narrated by David Attenborough, both series (2006 and 2016) were several years in the making. The astonishing footage of the planet's creatures and their environments was distributed to 130 countries around the world.

MOST LISTENED-TO RADIO

The everyday story of people living in a farming community, radio programme *The Archers* started in 1950 and is today the longest-running soap opera in any format anywhere in the world. Here are some of the other great radio programmes to have held the ear of the British public since the first national radio service was introduced in 1922.

Desert Island Discs: over 3,000 episodes have been recorded since Roy Plomley introduced actor and comedian Vic Oliver in 1942 as the first castaway.

Book at Bedtime: the John Buchan novel *The Three Hostages* was the first book to be read at bedtime in 1949, and the programme is still going strong.

The Goon Show: running from 1951 to 1960, this surreal comedy programme made household names of Spike Milligan, Harry Secombe, Peter Sellers and Michael Bentine.

Hancock's Half Hour: this 1950s sitcom had Tony Hancock playing a down-at-heel comedian living at the dilapidated 23 Railway Cuttings in East Cheam. A TV version was also aired.

Test Match Special: ball-by-ball cricket coverage was introduced in 1927 by the magnificently named head of BBC outside broadcasting Seymour de Lotbiniere and morphed into *Test Match Special* in 1957.

Just a Minute: chaired by Nicholas Parsons ever since it began in 1967, panellists must speak for a minute on a given subject 'without hesitation, repetition or deviation'.

I'm Sorry, I Haven't a Clue: introduced as 'the antidote to panel games', this sees two teams of comedians given silly things to talk about by the chairman (who was Humphrey Lyttelton from the programme's inception in 1972 until his death in 2008).

The Hitchhiker's Guide to the Galaxy: this science-fiction comedy introduced in 1978 follows the adventures of bumbling Englishman Arthur Dent and his friend Ford Prefect, an alien who writes for *The Hitchhiker's Guide to the Galaxy*.

Tips on how to be British today

It's not easy to be British, or English, Northern Irish, Scottish or Welsh for that matter, without being aware of the main cultural aspects necessary to blend in seamlessly as a native. This chapter provides you with all the tips you will ever need to get by, starting with the generic British things you need to know before moving on to the more specific things you need to know depending on which of the four home nations you find yourself in.

HOW TO PASS YOURSELF OFF AS BRITISH

 Begin all conversations with a reference to the weather.

 Queue in an orderly fashion for anything at all and marvel at how much you don't seem to mind.

 Nod politely when people from somewhere else in the country speak to you in a funny accent and pretend you understand what they're saying.

 Learn the words to the national anthem 'God Save the Queen' (and tweak it to 'God Save the King' if Prince Charles ever gets to have a go).

 Learn the words to 'Rule Britannia' and watch the Last Night of the Proms every year, whether you normally like classical music or not.

Remember that your favourite national dish is now curry, but you still have fish and chips on a Friday.

 Rejoice in the fact that your tiny island nation can finish second in the Olympics.

 Listen to the shipping forecast for no apparent reason.

 Always say 'sorry' if someone bumps into you, whether they meant it or not.

 Dunk a digestive biscuit in your tea safe in the knowledge that it's not bad manners.

 Tell anyone who'll listen that no one will ever be better than the Beatles.

 Panic and stay at home at the first sign of snow.

 Expect all other nationalities to understand English. If they don't, repeat yourself ever more loudly and slowly until they do.

IMAGE CREDITS

Cover images – Stonehenge © SH-Vector/Shutterstock.
com; Ship © Vera Petruk/Shutterstock.com; Engine
© Morphart Creation/Shutterstock.com; Crown
© Yurkina Alexandra/Shutterstock.com; Radio ©
ARTSIOM ZAYADSKI/Shutterstock.com; Shakespeare
© Nadya_Art/Shutterstock.com; Plane © Arkady
Zakharov/Shutterstock.com; Union Jack © charnsitr/
Shutterstock.com; Palace © Monkik/Shutterstock.com;
DNA © Alhovik/Shutterstock.com; Ballot box © Emo/
Shutterstock.com; Queen by Olga Zakharova; Teapot
© kaetana/Shutterstock.com; Sweet jar © Lomingo/
Shutterstock.com; Soldier © Morphart Creation/
Shutterstock.com; Watch © Siberica/Shutterstock.
com; Ligature © geen graphy/Shutterstock.com;

pp.8/9 – Queen © Paul Dymott/Shutterstock.com; map
© GEOATLAS - GRAPHI-OGRE/Shutterstock.com

pp.10/11 – Britannia © Perpedicular/
Shutterstock.com ; British Isles © GEOATLAS
- GRAPHI-OGRE/Shutterstock.com

pp.12/13 – British Isles © GEOATLAS - GRAPHI-OGRE/
Shutterstock.com; Islands by Olga Zakharova

pp.14/15 – Union Jack © NaughtyNut/Shutterstock.
com; Stonehenge © SH-Vector/Shutterstock.com

pp.16/17 – Figure on hill © grop/Shutterstock.
com; Crossed swords © Santi0103/Shutterstock.
com; Crown © Yurkina Alexandra/Shutterstock.
com; Celtic knots © Hoika Mikhail/Shutterstock.
com; Tree © y Sloth Astronaut/Shutterstock.com

p.18 – Wall © TroobaDoor/Shutterstock.
com; Temple © valeo5/Shutterstock.com;
Revellers © Elena Makeeva/Shutterstock.com;
Warriors © Thumbelina/Shutterstock.com

pp.20/21 – Feast © Morphart Creation/Shutterstock.
com; Sheep © Ivan Lukyanchuk/Shutterstock.com; Skull
© bazzier/Shutterstock.com; Warrior © Ron and Joe/
Shutterstock.com; Scribe © daseugen/Shutterstock.
com; Helmet © Gavris Sergey/Shutterstock.com

pp.22/23 – Viking © Le_Mon/Shutterstock.com;
Crown © N/A; Throne © Egor Shilov/Shutterstock.
com; Handshake © Tribalium/Shutterstock.
com; Fleurs de Lys crown © Yurkina Alexandra/
Shutterstock.com; Axe warrior © Shutterstock.com

pp.24/25 – Coin © Morphart Creation/Shutterstock.
com; Crown © Yurkina Alexandra/Shutterstock.com;
Windsor Castle © Artem Efimov/Shutterstock.com; Tower
of London © Artem Efimov/Shutterstock.com; Scottish
flag © bodrumsurf/Shutterstock.com; Book © okili77/
Shutterstock.com; Bow and arrow © SIM VA/Shutterstock.
com; Swords and shield © Ivan Baranov/Shutterstock.com

pp.26/27 – Pope © Sable Vector/Shutterstock.com;
Sword © Ivan Baranov/Shutterstock.com; Three lions ©
Billy Read/Shutterstock.com; Parchment © Nearbirds/
Shutterstock.com; Welsh dragon © Barry Barnes/

Shutterstock.com; Swords Ivan © Baranov/Shutterstock.
com; Rat © Snowboard School/Shutterstock.com;
Seal © Morphart Creation/Shutterstock.com

pp.28/29 – Battle scene © Vertyr/Shutterstock.
com; Spear © vonzur/Shutterstock.com

pp.30/31 © Durlo Hallmark/Shutterstock.com

pp.32/33 – Axe on block © Makc/Shutterstock.
com; Boy king © Eisfrei/Shutterstock.com; Torch
© Macrovector/Shutterstock.com; Queen by Olga
Zakharova; Ship © Vera Petruk/Shutterstock.com

pp.34/35 – Heart: musmellow/Shutterstock.
com; Axe on block: Makc/Shutterstock.com;
Tombstone: © Shutterstock.com; Barrel ©
ledokolua/Shutterstock.com; Ship © Vera Petruk/
Shutterstock.com; Cavalier © Shutterstock.com

pp.36/37 – Flag © AlexAlmighty/Shutterstock.com;
Axe on block © Makc/Shutterstock.com; Vagabond
© KenshiDesign/Shutterstock.com; Plum pudding:
Christos Georghiou/ Shutterstock.com; Rat © Snowboard
School/Shutterstock.com; Figures: N/A; Church ©
Pensiri/Shutterstock.com; Flame © Shutterstock.
com; House © Big Bann Studio/Shutterstock.com

pp.38 – King George by Olga Zakharova; Big Ben
© Sky Designs/Shutterstock.com; Maid © Rvector/
Shutterstock.com; Canadian flag © itiir/Shutterstock.
com; American flag © itiir/Shutterstock.com; Pistol ©
Shutterstock.com; French flag © itiir/Shutterstock.com

pp.40/41 – Napoleon © Ign/Shutterstock.
com; Telephone © Z-art/Shutterstock.com;
Factory © VikiVector/Shutterstock.com

pp.42/43 – Spanner and rail track © Shutterstock.
com; Gear: Mjosedesign/Shutterstock.com;
Polish flag © itiir/Shutterstock.com; Queen
© Paul Dymott/Shutterstock.com

pp.44/45 – Hay bale © miri019/Shutterstock.
com; Gigham pattern © newcorner/Shutterstock.
com; Clover © jitshutterstock/Shutterstock.
com; Hairbrush © petite lili/Shutterstock.com;
Noose © igor malovic/Shutterstock.com

pp.46/47 – King Edward by Olga Zakharova; Grapes
© Shutterstock.com; Coat of arms © amazonaws.
com; Handshake © Tribalium/Shutterstock.com

pp.48/49 – © wickerwood/Shutterstock.com; Soldiers
© ArtBitz/Shutterstock.com ; Plane © Vincze Szabi/
Shutterstock.com; Flag © itiir/Shutterstock.com

pp.50/51 – Ballot © ByEmo/Shutterstock.com; Virus ©
SilDim/Shutterstock.com; Building © Yevgen Lagunov/
Shutterstock.com; Flag © itiir/Shutterstock.com;
Commonwealth © Julinzy/Shutterstock.com; Hitler ©
rudall30/Shutterstock.com; Coin by Olga Zakharova

pp.52/53/54 – Soldiers © wickerwood/Shutterstock.
com; Planes © FabianGame/Shutterstock.com